WICCA
HAT'S THE REAL DEAL

Breaking through the Misconceptions

D1606354

• Dayna Winters • Patricia Gardner • Angela Kaufman •

Schiffer Publishing Ltd

4880 Lower Valley Road, Atglen, Pennsylvania 19310

Cover image by Dayna Winters using graphic elements from Anita Lee Creations
Ouija is a registered trademark of Parker Brothers, Inc.

Schiffer Books are available at special discounts for bulk purchases for sales promotions or premiums. Special editions, including personalized covers, corporate imprints, and excerpts can be created in large quantities for special needs. For more information contact the publisher:

Schiffer Publishing Ltd.
4880 Lower Valley Road
Atglen, PA 19310
Phone: (610) 593-1777; Fax: (610) 593-2002
E-mail: Info@schifferbooks.com

For the largest selection of fine reference books on this and related subjects,
please visit our website at **www.schifferbooks.com**
We are always looking for people to write books on new and related subjects. If you have an idea for a book please contact us at the above address.

This book may be purchased from the publisher. Include $5.00 for shipping.
Please try your bookstore first. You may write for a free catalog.

In Europe, Schiffer books are distributed by
Bushwood Books
6 Marksbury Ave.
Kew Gardens
Surrey TW9 4JF England
Phone: 44 (0) 20 8392 8585; Fax: 44 (0) 20 8392 9876
E-mail: info@bushwoodbooks.co.uk
Website: www.bushwoodbooks.co.uk

Copyright © 2011 by Dayna Winters, Patricia Gardner, Angela Kaufman
Text and photos by authors unless otherwise noted

Library of Congress Control Number: 2011930180

Designed by Stephanie Daughery
Type set in DeRoos/Book Antiqua

ISBN: 978-0-7643-3908-0
Printed in the United States of America

DEDICATION

To my loving husband, Mark, for being my inspiration, heart, love, soul mate, and a pillar of support in my life; and to my children, Josh, Matt, Mike, Jess, and Ty for making every day of my life one that is a unique balance of blessings, love, and endless surprises. To my coven sisters, friends, and co-authors, Patricia and Angela, for their friendship, support, and all the hard work they put forth in creating this book. To my coven brothers and friends in The Craft, Justyn and Sathish; to my parents for raising me with an inquisitive and open mind; and to the God and Goddess—thanks for all blessings big and small.

~Dayna Winters

I dedicate this book to my son, Phillip, who never cared that the world thought of me as bizarre and loved me anyway. To little Miss Isis for making me giggle everyday; to Dayna and Angela, who's strength and wisdom have brought this book to fruition; to Sathish and Justyn who are a part of our spiritual journey; and to the Goddess for guiding us every step of the way. Blessed Be.

~Patricia Gardner

This book is dedicated to Jim, my partner in all things; thank you for the love, support, and encouragement, and for respecting me and my beliefs from the beginning. To my parents and family for allowing me to explore new things without judgment, and to the coven: Pat, Dayna, Justyn, and Sathish for their mentoring and support. This book is also dedicated to the Goddess for the opportunity to be taught and challenged by the above mentioned, and for the opportunity to bring the truth to those who seek it.

~Angela Kaufman

ACKNOWLEDGMENTS

WE APPRECIATE THE INVALUABLE SUPPORT of our editor, Dinah Roseberry, who made herself readily available to answer all of our questions and who eased our minds through the book-writing process; we also appreciate the support of the entire staff at Schiffer Publishing. We are equally grateful for the assistance of author Dana D. Eilers for her tremendous help in addressing the legal aspects of Wicca and for reviewing our work. We are truly grateful for the support offered by sister Witch and author, Jo Lynne Gianvecchio-Valerie. We want to also thank Justyn Staley, our coven brother, for having to endure many class nights of teaching our young coven members as we took the time to research and write this book. Most of all, we are greatly appreciative of the support from all of our friends and loved ones. Last, but not least, we are thankful to the God and Goddess, for being blessed with such an amazing opportunity to share our knowledge with others.

CONTENTS

INTRODUCTION

*"A lie can travel halfway around the world
while the truth is putting on its shoes."*

~Mark Twain

W HEN ENCOUNTERING THE BOOK, *Wicca: What's the Real Deal?*, the reader might ask: Why another book on breaking through Wiccan misconceptions? With a number of books offered on the subject and free information on the Internet, why is it necessary to offer another book that attempts to destroy the myths associated with the practices of Witchcraft and Wicca? The answer is simple; serious misunderstandings still exist, even with the many resources available.

Almost every Wiccan encounters people who base their understandings of Witches on what they have read in fairy tales, on the Web, what they have seen on television or in movies, or on what someone with little to no knowledge of Wicca has told them. While there are many reliable materials about Wiccan practices available, there are an equal number of resources depicting Wiccans unfavorably. As Wiccans, we have encountered people who have some questionable ideas about what The Craft is, and what its practitioners represent; sometimes these misinformed individuals even hold influential positions in society.

Pervasive misconceptions about Wicca have forced many Wiccans to hide who they are; some practitioners refrain from telling their families, friends, colleagues, and associates the fact they are Wiccan. Some Wiccans are still hiding their beliefs, not because of shame, but because it is easier to keep their faith secret than it is to deal with the onslaught of questions, sneers, looks, and assumptions they will be forced to deal with when they reveal their chosen faith.

Many Wiccans find the preconceived notions people have frustrating, and they are equally tired of having to justify their beliefs. People view us as strange, bizarre, weird, dark, emotive, or eccentric because of our religious preferences. People shun us in public because they want nothing to do with Witches or individuals allegedly "deceived by the devil." Some criticize, label, and stereotype us. We are sometimes mocked, taunted, ridiculed, and insulted. At times, we are even the victims of vicious hate crimes and extreme acts of religious intolerance.

Many of the misconceptions about Witchcraft and Wicca are preposterous, and it is hard to imagine how anyone with a rational mind can believe such misconceptions at all; yet, these common misunderstandings persist. A quote attributed to Mark Twain suggests, *"A lie can travel halfway around the world while the truth is putting on its shoes."* Such is the case with the misconceptions about Wicca: People embrace erroneous understandings faster than the truth.

As the authors of this book, we feel this body of work with the aim of dispelling myths about Wicca is essential so perhaps more individuals can open their minds to the truth about something they might not completely understand. We offer no apologies for materials in this book that might otherwise seem redundant—some of the information presented herein bears repeating, since still so many do not understand what it means to be a practitioner of modern Witchcraft and Wicca.

We did not write this book to recruit Wiccans or to convert anyone to Wicca. This book is our attempt to change the world and to change some of the ways people perceive Wiccans. The reader of this work must determine what he or she believes about Witchcraft and Wicca; our hope is that this book proves to be an informative resource that one can use to expand one's horizons, clear up any confusion, and explain what it means to be Wiccan. If we can explain the truth about Wicca and The Craft to one person and he or she can walk away with a clear understanding of Wiccan beliefs and practices, then this book will have done its job. If we can promote understanding and religious tolerance, all of our hard work in putting this book together will have been more than worth the effort.

We offer here one final note to the reader; it has long been the convention in writing to use lowercase spellings when referring to a non-Judeo-Christian deity. We intentionally capitalize *God* and

Goddess throughout this work to make an important point: that our deities are as important to us as the God of monotheistic religions is to those that worship Him. We also intentionally capitalize the words *Witch, Pagan,* and *Witchcraft* whenever referencing a person who practices Magick and worships one or more deities. We lowercase *witch* and *pagan* to refer to individuals who practice Magick without conforming to a religion. We also capitalize *Magick*, and *The Craft* to specify the sacredness of the Magickal Arts.

~Dayna Winters, Patricia Gardner, and Angela Kaufman
Elders of the Dragon Warriors of ISIS

The Elders of the Dragon Warriors of Isis Coven in Upstate New York. Back row from left to right: Justyn Staley and Sathish Vijayan. Front row from left to right: Dayna Winters, Angela Kaufman, and Patricia Gardner.

CHAPTER 1

MISUNDERSTOOD TERMINOLOGY AND ERRONEOUS PERCEPTIONS

"All truth passes through three stages.
First, it is ridiculed.
Second, it is violently opposed.
Third, it is accepted as being self-evident."
~Arthur Schopenhauer

WHAT IS MODERN WITCHCRAFT ANYWAY? Isn't the practice of Witchcraft something sinful? Isn't Witchcraft merely make-believe? Are there *real* Witches in society today? Neophyte Wiccans, individuals interested in The Craft, and non-practitioners unsure about the legitimacy of Craft practices commonly pose all of the latter questions. Modern Witchcraft is a genuine practice, and Wiccans are just one group of people who practice it. So what is Wicca? What is a Witch, and what is Witchcraft? The roots of the words *Wicca, Witchcraft,* and *Witch* remain ambiguous, and an examination of the suggested etymological roots of the latter terms reveal multiple meanings.

Wicca is a religion: one serving as a guideline for a way of living one's life. According to Charles Godfrey Leland, *Wicca* also denotes "wisdom;" *Wicca* comes from *witga* meaning "a prophet, seer, magician, or sorcerer."[1] *Wicca* also comes from *wiccian:* a

A Witch's conical hat.

word with the same meaning as *vicca*. A comparison of the word *vicca* with *Wicca* suggests a Wiccan is a practitioner of the Magickal Arts: an art revered and honored as a sacred practice.[2] Meanwhile, Witchcraft is The Craft of the wise, since a craft is the act of applying knowledge, gained via study and experience, with strength, wisdom, and carefully honed skill.

A Witch is a practitioner of Witchcraft, and the word *Witch*, like the word *Wicca*, denotes "wisdom."[3] *Witch* has roots in *wicche* and *wicce*, meaning wizard or Witch.[4] Some references suggest the word *Witch* comes from the Gothio *veihan* meaning, "to consecrate."[5] There is also a link between the word *Witch* and *wicken* meaning "to predict," and *wizlian* or *wicheln* meaning "divinatory practices."[6] The word *Witch* comes from *wikken*, meaning to "Divine or soothsay," *wikkerske*, meaning "male or female soothsayer," as well as *wicklen* meaning, "to enchant."[7] The word *wician* meaning "to blink, to close and open one's eyes, or to bend one's self," also has connections to the word *Wiccan*.[8] The word *Witch* comes from the Anglo-Saxon terms *wit an* and *witan*, meaning "to see," and "to do," respectively.[9]

To summarize, a Witch is a wise person, a prophet, seer, and magician, one skilled in the art of sorcery, and one capable of consecration, divination, and enchantment. The terms *wit an* and *witan* imply that a Witch seeks to perceive ("to see") new, esoteric, and mundane understandings and to apply ("to do") what he or she learns. A *Witch* also has the ability to "bend one's self" via the process of shaping or focusing their will and energies to create outward manifestations of their desires in the mundane world. The idea of "bending one's self," can simultaneously mean reaching beyond the physical plane to planes wholly spiritual or working within astral realms.

The term *wician* implies that a Witch is an individual who at one time had his or her eyes closed to the mysteries, but through study, initiation, and enlightenment, the practitioner's eyes are "opened." Reflecting on the "Allegory of the Cave" in Plato's *The Republic*, the meaning of *wician* as "blink," and its relation to the practices of a Witch becomes clear. In the story, Socrates enters into a dialogue about the differences between illusion and reality. Chained prisoners who can see nothing but shadows on the wall of the cave, once freed, can turn and see the burning fire affixed behind them. The light of the flames temporarily blind the prisoners, the light illuminating reality or truth, until they perhaps "blink" several times and rub their eyes repeatedly so their eyes can adjust to the light they are seeing and the world it illuminates.[10] Plato's allegory can explain the neverending spiritual journey of the Wiccan.

Symbolically, blinking represents the act of looking outward into the world, taking in what one sees, closing one's eyes, and then reflecting inward. It also represents the maintenance and continual adjustment of one's focus. Through constant study, a Wiccan encounters new, mundane, and esoteric teachings. The practitioner's "intellectual eye," or mind perceives or sees (*wit an*) new understandings. Gradually, after a brief period of intellectual incubation, the mind then assimilates the new knowledge. Later, the practitioner can apply the newly attained wisdom "by doing" mundane or Magickal applications (*witan*), and this process continues throughout the practitioner's life. Living the Wiccan lifestyle is akin to living in a *quintessential state of marginality*: a practitioner continually moves between mundane and esoteric experiences, walks the fine line between both worlds, recognizes the natural ebb and flow between the two, and draws knowledge from all experiences. Living in the quintessential state of marginality allows the practitioner to experience the best of both realms and to draw more from their experiences for the betterment of his or her life.

The words Witch, Witchcraft, and Wicca are often misinterpreted by those who are outside of the pagan community. Various misconceptions and long-held beliefs have corrupted the true understanding of what it means to be a Wiccan practitioner of the Magickal Arts. In an effort to conquer some of the major misconceptions still so pervasive in society, presented here are some of the most common, sometimes preposterous, misconceptions people have about Wicca and Witchcraft. The following text includes the common myth and an explanation as to why each myth is misleading or altogether incorrect.

MISUNDERSTOOD TERMINOLOGY

MYTH: **All Pagans are practitioners of Witchcraft.**
TRUTH: *Many Pagans are not Witches, and Pagans follow a variety of different religious paths.*

The term *Pagan* comes from the post-classical Latin *paganus* meaning "villager;" as the use of the word evolved, *paganus* came to mean "heathen."[11]

Ancient Romans referred to people living in rural areas, those who were not easy to reach or easy to convert to Christianity, as Pagans. The Roman military used the word to refer to all people who were not military personnel.[12] Later, when the term "Christian soldiers" came into being, the word *pagan* came to mean all non-Christians.[13]

Presently, the term *pagan* represents all members of society following "the old ways," some form of "earth-based" religion, or individuals who do not conform to a society's major religions: This can include people adhering to Native American beliefs and Druidism, among other faith systems. The term also refers to a polytheist who centers their practice on the earth and nature. It is similar to proofs in geometry; in order to be a Wiccan, a practitioner must revere all of nature and worship the Goddess and/or God (some covens and solitary practitioners are strictly Goddess or God oriented). Similarly, in order to be Catholic, one must be a monotheistic Christian with a belief in Jesus Christ, but not all Christians are Catholic: there are also Protestants, Baptists, Lutherans, and so on. Wicca falls under the umbrella term *Pagan*, but the term *Pagan* does not solely define Wiccan Witches. While all Witches are Pagans, not every Pagan is a Witch and many Pagans do not practice Witchcraft.

MYTH: **Wiccans are part of a cult, and the words "occult" and "cult" mean the same thing.**
TRUTH: *People often confuse the term* **cult** *with the term* **occult**.

When speaking of the Magickal Arts, the word *occult* means "secret, concealed, or hidden."[14] Learning about the occult is the act of studying things defined as paranormal, supernatural, and spiritual and the gaining of hidden or secret knowledge from such studies. In contrast, the word *cult* has two distinct meanings. To understand the difference between *a cult* and the *occult*, it becomes necessary to examine what cults are and what they do.

A "cult," in an archaic sense, defines a group worshipping one or more deities.[15] Historians documenting the religious practices of different cultures have described religious "cults": groups paying reverence to specific deities or holy figures. For example, there was the Dianic cult in ancient Rome, the Dionysian cult in Greece, the Osirian and Isiac cults in ancient Egypt, and there was even the cult of the Virgin Mary in the Middle Ages. The latter cults were a collection of people dedicated to worshipping a particular deity or holy figure, and the cult members' reverence illustrated extreme devotion to the figure worshipped.

Today, the word *cult* carries a different connotation. The modern understanding of the term defines a group with atypical, disturbing, and harmful beliefs.[16] A cult is a group led by one to several enigmatic leaders who have full control over the organization. Cult leaders often forbid members from questioning anything. Isolation from friends and family is often encouraged, and sometimes cults may use deceptive measures for recruiting purposes. Methods such as mind control are common in a cult. Members are not encouraged to think for themselves, and they are often encouraged to rely solely on the direction of the cult leader or other cult members. Independence and self-reliance are discouraged, and cult leaders will sometimes demand blind faith from group members. On occasion, cult leaders even take some or all of the worldly possessions belonging to their members as well.

If viewing Wicca as a "cult" in a positive and archaic sense where worshippers venerate one or more deities or Divine beings, then Wicca falls under the umbrella definition. If considering the definition of the term *cult* in its more modern and negative sense, then the opposite is true. Some Wiccans are solitary practitioners and cannot be a member of a cult since they are practicing alone and they answer to no one except themselves and the Divine. As for Wiccan coven members, they are also not involved in cults if they have joined a legitimate coven. While a coven may have a hierarchy consisting of a High Priest or High Priestess who rule over the coven and there are rules to adhere to in every group, at no time do the rules and regulations make the coven a cult. Rules exist within a coven in order to keep the group organized and united. Legitimate coven leaders and members encourage people to ask questions, to think for themselves, and they encourage the maintenance of familial and social connections. In or outside of a coven, practitioners offer reverence to one or more deities. While a practitioner honors the High Priest and High Priestess for the spiritual guidance they offer, the Witch does not worship them; instead, the practitioner views the High Priest or High Priestess as the embodiment of the God and Goddess.

Spiritual coven leaders lead and teach by example. Wiccans do not recruit others to join a coven, and do not seek to control the minds of others. There are no demands for the personal property of coven members at any time, and the only things coven leaders expect of members is their dedication to the practice of Witchcraft, their studies, learning, and the sacrifice of some of their personal time for the purposes of spiritual development. Wiccans honor the earth and worship of the Divine above the words or actions of any mortal. If a practicing Wiccan feels that a coven leader and its members are beginning to behave in a cult-like manner, then he or she is encouraged to leave the organization, to seek out a different coven, or to continue practicing The Craft as a solitary until a reputable and trustworthy coven is located.

MYTH: **The spelling of Magick with a "k" is incorrect.**
TRUTH: *In the past, the word magic has taken on a number of meanings depending upon its context.*

"Magic" is an art form used for healing, something to exploit for good fortune or it is a myth; it is a false promise used to con the desperate; or it is a practice of illusion and trickery. It is entertainment or fun for children or it describes an impossible feat: one that a person aspires to, but can never obtain; the uses for the term *magic* have so many subtle meanings, none of which reflects what the term *Magick* means to the Wiccan practitioner.

Within the Wiccan faith, there has been an attempt to clarify so many of the myths and misunderstandings that have kept Witchcraft and *Magickal* practices on the outskirts of wide public acceptance. One of the many areas that modern Witches have attempted to offer major damage control is around the public perception of what it means to practice the Magickal Arts. In order to separate the reference to a serious working based on focusing the intent of the practitioner and projecting energy to create a desired result, from magic involving trickery or illusion, it is a common practice to add a "k" at the end of the term *magic*.

The original term magic had several different spellings in Middle English, and the first appearance of the word occurs around the 1300s in the Old French magique, meaning magical.[17] In the late 1390s, the term appears in the works of Geoffrey Chaucer as magik, and magike.[18] In the early 1590s, poet and playwright Christopher Marlowe used the term as Magicke in his play *The Tragicall History of the Life and Death of Doctor Faustus*. In the late 1720s, Daniel DeFoe used the word Magick in his work: A Compleat System of Magick; or a History of the Black Arts, when defining occult practices.[19] By the late 1780s, magic became a standard spelling for the term, until the late 1920s when Aleister Crowley, the famed occultist, renewed the use of the term Magick in his work, *Magick in Theory and Practice*.[20] Thus, the use of the term Magick is not a spelling error; the spelling differentiates between occult-related practices and sleight of hand or stage magic. However, not every occultist, Witch, Pagan, or writer relies on the use of the term Magick, and the people often interchange the two terms.

MYTH: Witchcraft and Wicca are a "New Age" religion.
TRUTH: *As mentioned earlier, Wicca and Witchcraft are not the same.*

Wicca is a religion, practiced by Witches, which incorporates the use of Magick coupled with the religious worship of one or more deities. Witchcraft is the study and application of Magick, with or without a religious structure. The term "New Age" describes a new and enlightened mode of understanding, and it encompasses a variety of religions. It also describes a historical movement as well as a movement away from widely accepted Western religious ideals toward the acceptance of unconventional theologies and ideologies from various cultures. In the latter sense, Wicca does seem to fall under the umbrella term of "New Age."[21] In contrast, Wiccan practices are rooted in the "old religions" of Europe before Christianity dominated European cultures. Therefore, the religion is not really a "new" religious movement, but rather the reemergence of older religious practices.

Some people will argue that Wicca is a relatively novel religion started by Gerald Gardner, but the understandings of Wicca come from religious beliefs far older than the emergence of Gardnerian Wicca in the 1950s: just one of many Wiccan traditions. The earliest peoples revered a Goddess. Ancient temples dedicated to the Goddess exist all over the world. Paganism pre-dominated the world over, and the ancient concepts of spirituality in Wicca are parallel to various ancient pre-monotheistic religions. While Wiccan practitioners do embrace some of the practices, beliefs, and understandings commonly explored by people interested in New Age philosophies, such as the use of crystals, holistic healing methods, astrology, natural sciences, quantum physics, and other concepts, casting the Wiccan religion under the umbrella definition of "New Age," seems to limit the religion's scope. The term "New Age," proves all together misleading. To consider Wicca as a "New Age" religion invalidates the religion's ancient roots.

MYTH: **A coven and a covenant are the same.**
TRUTH: *To consider Wicca or Witchcraft as a "New Age" religion invalidates the ancient roots of the religion and practice.*

Covenant, in one instance defines the promise between the Christian God and humankind, and in another, refers to a contract or an agreement. In addition, sometimes the words *coven* and *covenant* are confused since they both come from the Latin *convenire*, meaning to gather, to unite, or to assemble.[22] To confuse the word *covenant* with *coven* suggests that one is thinking of the "agreement" or mythical "pact" that Witches allegedly make with the devil in exchange for supernatural powers. Wiccans do not make a pact or oath with any evil entity or being; the only oaths made by Wiccans involve honoring the Divine in all things and the pledge to "harm none."

The word *coven* defines a group of Witches consisting of three or more individuals who celebrate the sabbats (rituals celebrating the seasons), esbats (full moon rituals), perform Magickal workings together, and serve as a spiritual support system for one another. A coven may have a limit of thirteen members, but some have smaller or larger memberships. For covens that limit membership to thirteen practitioners, it is up to the High Priest or High Priestess of the coven to determine if hiving off is permissible. When a High Priest or High Priestess allows a coven to hive off, a Priest or Priestess from the existing group becomes the leader of the smaller group derived from the first. The new branch is a clan or grove. However, not every Wiccan practitioner becomes a member of a coven. Many practitioners of the faith prefer to remain solitary practitioners. For anyone interested in finding a local coven, one can visit *The Witches' Voice* website for a worldwide listing of covens. Information on how to access *The Witches' Voice* online is available in the resources section at the end of this book.

MYTH: The word "Witch" is so derogatory that it is better to use the word "Wiccan" when speaking to or about a follower of the Wiccan faith.

TRUTH: *When someone is referring to a Wiccan practitioner, the words Wiccan and Witch are both perfectly acceptable references.*

Many Wiccans are proud to use both terms. The word "Witch" is not derogatory, unless one uses it in a derogatory sense. When a person holds no understanding of what it means to be a Witch and uses the word in a condescending fashion, then it becomes something that is derisive and contemptuous. Many Wiccans appreciate the title of "Witch," are proud to be called a Witch, and are honored to be counted as one of many Witches in society today. In fact, to use the term *Witch* in its correct sense, as a word indicating a person who practices a nature-based religion, worships one or more deities and strives for proficiency in the Magickal Arts, is the act of reclaiming the power of the word and its use. However, some Witches prefer the word *Wiccan* and refrain from using the word *Witch* when identifying themselves, for personal reasons.

MYTH: A male Witch is a warlock.

TRUTH: *Wiccans are Witches whether they are male or female.*

Satanists call a female practitioner a witch. Sometimes Satanic practitioners refer to a male practitioner as a warlock, depending upon the degree of the initiate. The word *war* comes from the Old French *wërr* meaning fury, and *wërran* meaning to create chaos and disorder.[23] The word lock originates from the Old English *loga* meaning "liar." The word warlock stems from the Old English *wǽloga* meaning "traitor," the Old Saxon *wârlogo*, and the Old English *wǽr* meaning "agreement or faith."[24] The latter etymology suggests that a warlock is someone who acts vengefully, creates disorder or chaos, uses deceit in Magickal practices, and is one who is "a traitor" of a particular faith. Early Christians would identify all male witches as warlocks because they believed them to be traitors of the Christian faith. Male Wiccans do not refer to themselves as warlocks; as mentioned earlier, Wiccans are Witches whether they are male or female. Wiccans do not worship the devil, make pacts with Satan, intentionally break oaths, intentionally deceive others, or use Magick for chaotic, disorderly, or harmful purposes. Many male Wiccans feel insulted when referred to as warlocks because of the term's negative connotations.

Myth: The Witching Hour, also known as the devil's hour, is at midnight.

Truth: *The notion of the Witching Hour seems to differ from one person to the next.*

Some people identify the "Witching Hour" as a single hour or several hours between eleven o'clock at night and six o'clock in the morning. Most commonly, the Witching Hour is identified as midnight: This marks a "between time" as the day transitions into a new day. Technically, if one were to identify "between times," or transitional hours of the day as a "Witching Hour," then it would be logical to assume that dawn, noon, and dusk, would also be considered "Witching Hours," as well. Taken to an extreme, every hour of the day is transitional, thus, a practitioner could consider each hour of the day as a "between time." Some people believe that the Witching Hour only occurs at midnight on the night of a full moon. Meanwhile, some assert that it occurs from one to three o'clock in the morning. At this time, many are asleep and psychic awareness and intuitive communications are at their height. Some people believe the Witching Hour ranges from three to six o'clock in the morning: the darkest hours before the dawn of a new day.

A practitioner therefore defines the ideal Witching Hour, a special time of power, for Magickal workings; some practitioners suggest that the hour is an ideal time to hold esbats, but Wiccans can hold esbats at any hour of the evening when the full moon appears.

The Witching Hour is not the same thing as the "demonic witching hour" or the "devil's hour," a time with Christian undertones. The devil's hour is 3am, a time viewed as an inversion and mockery of 3pm on Good Friday: This is when some believe Jesus Christ died on the cross. The time of 3am is also a mockery of the Trinity.

In fact, 3am may also serve as an inversion of the final hour of None: one of the canonical hours of the Church. Ancient Grecians and Romans divided night and day into four equal parts, each part containing three hours. None is the hours from 12pm to 3pm. None comes from the Latin *nonus* meaning "ninth."[25] This refers to the fact that the first hour of None is the ninth hour following dawn. The final hour of None (3pm), is not only associated with Christ's death, but Saint John Cassian identified the hour with Christ's descent into the regions of hell.[26] Thus, an inversion of 3pm would occur at three o'clock in the morning and with an inversion of meaning, would prove a symbolic representation of evil's ascent from hell and its release onto the earthly plane. Interestingly, many paranormal reports consisting of negative activity occur right around three o'clock in the morning.

ERRONEOUS PERCEPTIONS

MYTH: All witches follow the Wiccan religion.
TRUTH: *Not every Witch is Wiccan.*

Wiccans may interchange the words *Witch* and *Wiccan* freely. In addition, many people from different cultures identify with the term *witch*, but do not follow the Wiccan religion. Thus, not every Witch is Wiccan. For example, Satanists call themselves witches, but they do not adhere to Wiccan principles. Likewise, some people practice syncretic religions that involve the merging of seemingly paradoxical beliefs. In addition, some people become well versed in the Magickal Arts, and perform spells, divination, dowsing, and healing Arts without conforming to any form of religious structure.

As liberal as Wicca's structure is, some people choose to practice Witchcraft without giving reverence to a God or Goddess or without observing religious holidays. The word *witch* has a meaning that has expanded over time; it has become a catchall term for people who have a variety of religious beliefs, or none at all, but who are proficient at the Magickal Arts. Wicca, on the other hand, is a religion in which the Magick and "fun stuff" is just a small part of living a Wiccan lifestyle. A Wiccan does not center their practices on spells and dabbling in whatever occult-salad they choose just for entertainment or for the sole purposes of personal gain. Wiccans see the religion as a calling, and even the Magickal work, divination, and healing Arts are undertaken in the greater context of a religion: one that emphasizes spiritual growth and the evolution of the soul.

MYTH: There are Witches in all religions.
TRUTH: *There are Witchcraft practitioners in various religious groups, but there are not Witches in all religious systems.*

For example, there are no Jehovah Witnesses or Born-Again Christians practicing Witchcraft since their religious systems involve an adamant belief in the evil of Magick. Meanwhile, many cultures believe in witches and witchcraft, but the understanding of what witches do and what they represent differs greatly from culture to culture. Sometimes superstition or misogynistic views shape a culture's understandings about witches and such beliefs have nothing to do with the more modern understandings of Witchcraft; as a result, many unique cultural understandings of what witches are do not relate to Wicca or its practitioners.

Religions that fuse paradoxical beliefs or practices are syncretic religions. These religions aim at reconciling opposing principles in religion and combine the use of Magick with a religious system that sometimes frowns upon its use. Some examples of syncretic religions include Curanderismo, Hoodoo, Santería, and Voudou, among others. To a certain degree, many religions contain adaptations of other religious practices and beliefs. The transmogrification of Pagan holidays, beliefs, and traditions follows the rise of Christianity; the result is the adoption, adaptation, and vilification of sacred days, Pagan beliefs, and iconology. The assimilation of Pagan beliefs and Christian understandings led to easier Pagan to Christian conversions.

Presently, a relatively new movement in The Craft exists involving some practitioners who are attempting to merge Christian and Wiccan practices, and the prospect of merging the two religious belief systems remains a subject of heavy debate. Witchcraft is the practice of Magick, and Wicca is a nature/God and Goddess-based religion including ancient Magickal practices. Some people claim to be Witches and Christian: This argument is at odds with Wiccan and Christian understandings. Biblical verse and Christian teachings forbid polytheistic practices as in Exodus 20:3: "You shall have no other gods before me."[27] This teaching is repetitious and appears in the Bible in Exodus 23:12, and in Deuteronomy 6:14, as well as other verses. Myriad biblical verses prove problematic for a practitioner of Witchcraft with Christianity, a religion involving monotheistic practices.

The Bible also has writings that are clearly against the use of Magick and Witchcraft; in Deuteronomy 18:9-11, the Bible suggests that a Christian should not participate in the use of divination, Magick, Witchcraft, spell casting, or communication with spirits and familiars.[28] Bear in mind, Gnostics follow different tenets than those in the canonical Bible and some may engage in Magickal undertakings. Throughout history, individuals have also used Magick and attempted to unify Cabalistic, Hermetic, and Christian teachings. Therefore, there have been efforts to unify the practices of Magick and Christianity throughout history. There are also individuals that practice Angel Magick. Nevertheless, to say one is a Witch and that he or she adheres to the teachings of the Christian Bible is to assert seriously conflicting beliefs.

MYTH: Wicca is a fad people outgrow. It is a spiritual trend spreading across the globe.

TRUTH: *The Wiccan path is not for everyone. Those who find the Wiccan path fulfilling do not outgrow their faith.*

If a practitioner follows this path with a true heart, the individual grows with knowledge, and gains a greater awareness of the world and his or her role within it. A person improves his or her focus when living the Wiccan lifestyle, and can make wonderful, magickally-aligned changes in his or her life. As an earth-based religion that stems from pre-Christian religious thought and practices having survived for thousands of years, this invalidates the notion that Wicca is a fad.

While some people might become involved in Wicca only to later give up the path or to convert to another religion, this does not make Wiccan practices a fad. What it means is that people are prone to changing their minds: Their beliefs, and their actions then follow suit. When a person leaves a church or synagogue, it does not mean that the church or synagogue no longer stands as a place that offers religious services and support because one or more people decide to leave. Under the same notion, when a person develops an interest in Wicca it should not be assumed that the Wiccan faith system is a fad or something they are "trying on." After all, Wicca is a legitimate religion, not a pair of leg warmers or a cool looking pair of jeans.

MYTH: Wicca is not a real religion; practitioners improvise religious practices.

TRUTH: *The Wiccan religion brings a new way of handling spirituality which many are not accustomed to; there are rules and a framework that unite practitioners in some basic beliefs and ethical considerations, coupled with a great deal of flexibility.*

The adherence to Wicca involves specific, religious codes of conduct, but the otherwise openness to individual spiritual experience causes some to view Wicca as a "self-created" religion. Adherence to the Wiccan Rede and some good common sense are essential in Wiccan practices, especially when using Magick. Yet, even with adherence to the Wiccan Rede, there is room for individual adaptation.

The flexibility of Wicca allows for the adaptation of some religious practices, but the religion is not entirely self-created. For example, some practitioners use parts from different spells or rituals in order to create a single spell or rite that they can perform alone or in a coven working. Of course, the rite or spell must still contain the components that are necessary, and the practitioner still performs the rite or spell at the appropriate time with the appropriate methods. However, the practitioner can easily adapt spells and ritual workings to suit individual preference. The knowledge of why one is performing the spell or ritual is the first part of the process, the intent of honoring the Divine and attuning one's self with nature is still the basis for the celebration when it comes to a ritual working, and spells still consist of necessary Magickal components. What's more, customizing a spell or ritual allows the rite to become more meaningful for the practitioner: This intensifies the practitioners' intent and lends power to the working.

Some may confuse the flexibility of Wiccan practices with complete laxity, but this is not the case. For instance, imagine a new practitioner, not yet versed in The Craft who decides to perform a holiday rite because the practitioner has viewed a television show that mentions Samhain as a Witches' holiday. Imagine that the individual has no idea why Witches celebrate Samhain, and the practitioner fails to prepare for the ritual working. In this imagined example, the practitioner also lacks a basic understanding of The Craft, but assumes that Wicca is a free and open religion. What can a little dabbling hurt? Now imagine that the individual improvises an entire ceremony, with no knowledge of circle casting, with no understanding of how important it is to honor the Divine, with no knowledge pertaining to the role of the elements, and with no knowledge of ritual tools and their use. At best, it is safe to say that in this scenario, the individual would have an experience almost completely absent of spiritual meaning. At worst, the individual may attract energies that he or she does not know how to deal with because they dabbled and attempted to use rites beyond their wisdom and understanding.

Clearly, a difference exists between having a solid understanding of a belief system, but being flexible enough to incorporate different and sometimes modern, practices of that faith, as opposed to getting a few concepts together and deciding to self-create the rest.

MYTH: All television shows accurately portray Wiccans.
TRUTH: *Most television shows inaccurately portray Wiccans.*

Television shows are all about ratings. You can count on the fact that what shows depict has little to do with reality or truth in most cases. Sometimes television shows portray Wiccans as evil or ignorant, and many Wiccans find nothing more irritating! Whether the television show is fiction or a "true-to-life" documentary, when shows portray Wiccans, someone is bound to walk away from such shows believing all the wrong things about Wicca and The Craft. Responsible, intelligent, ethical Wiccans are not evil. They do not mess around with dark forces or use Magick irresponsibly. Wicca is a religion promoting wisdom and education. Many Wiccans spend their lives studying and learning esoteric principles. They understand that knowledge is equivalent to power, and they retain an undying curiosity about the universe. Many Wiccans believe that one's lifetime is a time where the practitioner experiences a series of lessons, and the main reason for one's existence is to learn and to experience ("to see" and "to do"); it is through the neverending process of learning that Wiccans expand their understanding of themselves and their relationship to the Divine.

It is absurd to assume that one is familiar with an entire religious belief system that penetrates down to a lifestyle and culture because they saw it on television! After all, why does a favorite book never fully translate into a movie or television show? Film and television are only able to portray a glimpse of a larger system. Sometimes that small glimpse is incredibly inaccurate or fictionalized for dramatic purposes. It is all too easy to assume the one-dimensional view of a culture or religion represents the true basis of the belief system. Fictionalized television shows tell a story. Characters in the story personify common stereotypes and idiosyncrasies. Such portrayals are not the embodiment of all Wiccans. Specifically, television shows often portrays all Witches as evil, crazy, or as "tree hugging airheads." Some even masterfully combine the latter three. To assume that such depictions are remotely accurate is untrue. It undermines the vast array of diverse personalities, lifestyles, and Wiccan practices. Even "fact-based" documentaries can get it wrong.

MYTH: Wiccans are eccentric people with unusual beliefs.
TRUTH: *Many Wiccans are free thinkers, open-minded, and independent, but such qualities do not necessarily translate into being eccentric.*

Eccentric seems to be one of the top terms used to describe Wiccans, and the term *bizarre* comes in at a close second. To those who are not familiar with Wicca, its beliefs, traditions, and values, some of the beliefs associated with the religion may seem, at first, unusual. Wiccans believe in things like spirits, other worldly realms, karma, the neverending effort of defining one's role within the universe, and interacting with all in the universe in positive ways. The terms *eccentric* and *bizarre* are subjective and up for personal interpretation, but it needs to be made clear that just because a person's beliefs are different than another's, it does not mean that the person is weird, bizarre, or not "normal." Finally, being eccentric, odd, or bizarre is not a prerequisite for being Wiccan.

MYTH: **Most Witches are uneducated.**
TRUTH: *There are Wiccan attorneys, authors, doctors, police officers, teachers, researchers, and average individuals who are highly educated.*

Part of being a Wiccan involves the lifelong learning process since Wiccans believe that one of the main reasons for existence is for learning the life lessons one needs to master. Many Wiccans are interested in learning, in academics, in reading, in writing, and in learning about people, nature, and the world. To be a Wiccan involves a tremendous amount of study. Oftentimes, the mastering of the tenets, beliefs, and practices of the religion begin with reading a variety of books on the subject, and the practitioner's evolution as a spiritual being is highly dependent on continued education and exploration. Many Wiccans place equal value on knowledge derived from observations of the natural world, in addition to knowledge gained through academic studies.

MYTH: **Wiccans are psychologically unstable or they suffer from mental illness.**
TRUTH: *Wiccan beliefs may differ from other beliefs, but otherwise healthy Wiccans are fully functioning members of society.*

It is important to realize that what it is to be "normal" is a subjective concept; what one subculture finds perfectly acceptable in terms of beliefs and behaviors, another subculture may find repulsive or unacceptable. It is also important to realize that just because people partake of different practices, whether religiously oriented or not, it does not mean that they are mentally ill or that something is wrong with them.

Wiccans believe in Magick, but this belief does not disrupt their ability to communicate, form relationships, and function in society, barring any individual idiosyncrasies. Some Wiccans are solitary practitioners with strong relationships outside of familial connections; some Wiccans are members of covens with equally strong social and familial relationships, some practitioners have children, and the majority of Wiccans have little difficulty in establishing lasting relationships. Wiccan beliefs may differ from other beliefs, but otherwise healthy Wiccans are fully functioning members of society, and their spirituality gives them strength. Witches extend their awareness beyond the tangible, physical world in order to perceive and explore many layers of consciousness, just as many other people with different religious orientations have throughout the course of history.

Of course, Wiccans are human beings and as such, they are fallible; this means that it is possible for someone with a Wiccan religious-orientation to suffer from the same bio-psyche-social ailments that any human being can be afflicted with at any time. Mental illness affects all kinds of people. A religion is not a net or catching mitt for people suffering from mental disorders. Wiccans experience a wide range of emotions just like everyone else, and just as they are in no way immune to physical diseases, they are also not immune to mental illnesses. Yet, just because a Wiccan can sometimes face the challenge of a mental illness, it does not mean that when a mental illness presents itself that it stems from the practitioner's religious preferences or vice versa. More information on mental illness versus Magickal understandings is available in Chapter 4 of this book.

MYTH: **Wiccans enter into their spiritual path with the hopes of elevating their status in society or to develop a sense of self-importance.**

TRUTH: *There are many Wiccans who are capable, competent, responsible, and productive members of society. Wiccans work, go to school, raise families, and share their lives with friends and loved ones.*

In truth, many people even know one or more Wiccans and are not even aware of it! Wiccans are not strange or bizarre, and they usually do not have any extreme identifying markers that indicate their beliefs (unless one happens to spot a few pentacles)! Wiccans do not enter into their spiritual path with the hopes of elevating their status in society; in fact, they can face discrimination that results in the opposite effect, and their self-confidence is not dependent on whether or not the rest of the world knows that they are practitioners. While being Wiccan can prove fulfilling for both heart and soul, it is not the sole reason for becoming Wiccan. Witches participate as solitary practitioners or attend coven gatherings regularly, celebrate esbats monthly, celebrate sabbats eight times a year, focus on daily spiritual development, and enter into an endless journey of learning and discovery.

MYTH: **If you become a Wiccan, you will be able to learn Magick and all your friends will think you're cool.**

TRUTH: *Becoming a Wiccan and learning how to practice Magick is not a decision that should be ego-driven, and it is definitely not the way to win a popularity contest!*

When a person decides to become a Wiccan, he or she will eventually partake in Magickal practices. Seeing the positive results one can generate when using Magick can be exciting. However, the decision to learn about and use Magick should not have anything to do with how one's future Magickal abilities will make them look. The use of Magick is a serious endeavor, one that involves mastering the basics in order to establish a strong foundation in Magickal principles. Performing Magick is not about performing parlor tricks. It is not about impressing or shocking others. While using Magick enhances one's physical and spiritual life, it is not a method for helping a person climb a social ladder. If a person is really seeking to obtain the admiration of his or her friends, the individual should make the decision to be someone who is truly a good friend. Behaving in honorable ways, seeing all the beauty in life, sharing one's blessings, and becoming an individual who is a pillar of support for others, is what will make a person truly "cool" in the eyes of friends and family.

MYTH: **If you are a real Witch and you can use Magick, then your life should be perfect.**

TRUTH: *No one should assume that any living thing could live a perfect life.*

Besides, who decides what is "perfect," and what is not? In a sense, being a Wiccan means that one's life *is* "perfect." Every part of one's life has unfolded under the care of the God and Goddess and even the mistakes or challenges that have occurred in one's life have happened just as they needed to happen. Witches are not supposed to rely on Magick for personal gain or for the purposes of greed. A Witch's lifetimes are for learning. If everything were perfect, what would the practitioner learn in this life or the next? Witches experience just as many bumps in their journey as anyone else. Wiccans have jobs, families, and they worry about the same things other people do. Wiccans experience the hard times in a down economy as painfully as others, and some work in mundane jobs like other productive individuals in society. Some Wiccans raise children and worry just like every other loving parent, and their problems are no less a hardship than the problems anyone might experience at any given time. Life is perfect only when a person embraces all of the imperfections that come with it. That's what makes life an adventure.

MYTH: **Teenagers who are Wiccan are being rebellious.**

TRUTH: *Some teenagers might be rebelling by choosing the Wiccan path; others may be sincere about wanting to learn The Craft and live a Wiccan lifestyle.*

In order to determine if a teen's interest in Wicca is serious or frivolous, a person should take the opportunity to bond with the teenager and find out why they are interested in Wicca. With tenets such as "harm none," and with actions that involve honoring the Earth, the Goddess, and the God, it is safe to say that Wicca might be the best thing that could ever happen to some teens. A fast method for finding out if a teen holds a serious interest in Wicca or is interested in it for the shock value, would be to support the teen's interests in the religion. If the teen is just rebelling, he or she will lose interest quickly. If the teen is serious about Wicca, it will be easier to support and validate the child's beliefs if one is able and willing to learn about the belief system as well.

Some teens demonstrate an interest in Wicca just to be rebellious, but this does not explain every teen's interests. Some teens seeking Wiccan teachers contact covens, but the coven leaders will not teach teenagers that are less than eighteen years of age or may demand parental consent. The reason that some covens choose to request parental consent is that the coven elders do not want to infringe upon the rights of parents to raise their children the way they see fit. Some coven leaders feel that teens are not ready to learn the mysteries until they have reached the age of consent. In contrast, some Pagan Elders teach teens about The Craft without parental consent or without the expectation that the individual be of a certain age before undertaking esoteric studies.

Teenagers are often interested in Wicca because they see in the religion what many adults miss: the open connection to the universe and the connection to Mother Earth and all life. Some people, after becoming Wiccan, develop the sense of "coming home," a deep sense of belonging, and an even deeper sense of spiritual fulfillment. Wicca is not a catchall religion for the rebellious. Since teenagers are just beginning to explore who they are, it is not surprising that Wicca proves an attractive option: The religion is a system of belief that helps an individual on the neverending journey of self-discovery. With the latter notion in mind, consider that serious Pagan teachers expect a degree of discipline and dedication to studies that a rebellious teen is unlikely to demonstrate. In a serious coven or under the tutelage of a strict mentor, a teen with insincere interest is likely to lose interest quickly.

MYTH: **Wiccans are a bad influence on small children and teenagers.**
TRUTH: *The Wiccan religion does not promote any practices that are harmful or destructive to adults, children, animals, or the world.*

The positive principles of the Wiccan faith include things like the strength derived from spirituality, self-respect, respect for others and the environment, the care for the world and all within it, balance in all things, honor, and integrity. Teens in Pagan-oriented groups and in a variety of more traditional youth groups learn about the latter-mentioned concepts. What's more, the tenets of Wicca promote environmentalist ideals and these ideals do not negatively influence children and young adults.

Some Wiccans are parents and some are not. Some Wiccans work with children, others do not. At no time do responsible Wiccans intentionally attempt to steer a child or teen in the wrong direction on his or her life's path. This stereotype stems from unreasonable fears that Wiccans are out to convert everyone they meet. In addition, sometimes a person is afraid of the moment when an impressionable individual encounters a Witch, that the practitioner will purposely persuade or entice the young individual to develop interests in the occult and that such interests are sinister, sinful, or spiritually dangerous. In truth, no ethical Wiccan makes an effort to convert anyone. A Witch does not promote the irresponsible use of Magick, and being Wiccan does not make someone a bad role model or influence. Of course, there are exceptions to the rule. A Wiccan can make bad decisions that can later result in the individual serving as a poor role model for young people. For more information, see the section Teens and Wicca in Chapter 4.

MYTH: Witchcraft is the practice of seeking spiritual guidance from any other source than God.

TRUTH: *Wiccans seek guidance from the Divine in the form of a God and a Goddess: two halves of a single Divine source. They see the Divine in all living things and all of nature.*

Just because Wiccans do not search for guidance from the God of monotheistic religions, it does not mean that they do not seek guidance from the Divine, as Wiccans perceive it. Wiccans also seek guidance from spiritual ancestors, from physical and spiritual teachers, and from spirit guides. The deities Wiccans seek guidance from are in every form of the natural cycle and in every part of the earth. Wiccans do not see the God and Goddess as separate. They exist and course through all things. Wiccans seek guidance from the wise, from friends, from family, and always know that they can turn to the Mother Goddess and the God when seeking spiritual guidance.

Wiccans see the Divine in all living things and in all of nature. Cohoes Falls in Upstate New York.

MYTH: Wiccans are solely women or gay men.

TRUTH: *There is no mandate on sexual orientation and being a homosexual is not a prerequisite in order to be welcomed in the Wiccan community.*

While the Wiccan religion is primarily a Goddess-oriented religion, Wiccans also give reverence to the Masculine Divine. Since Wiccans see the natural polarity and Divine energies in all things, the Wiccan religion is not solely for women. While it is true that there are covens that, by choice, do not allow male practitioners, there are just as many, if not more covens that welcome male coven members. What's more, there is no mandate on sexual orientation and being a homosexual is not a prerequisite in order to be welcomed in the Wiccan community. There is no Wiccan doctrine prohibiting homosexuality; many Wiccans are accepting of gay Witches; they fully support their rights, and the Wiccan community tends to welcome all men interested in walking the Wiccan path, no matter what their sexual orientation.

MYTH: As Witches get deeper into the occult, they partake of drinking, drugs, and sex.

TRUTH: *The Wiccan faith does not promote the use of illegal drugs, the abuse of alcohol, the abuse of legal drugs, or an overzealous, out-of-control approach to sexual practices.*

While some practitioners use wine or alcohol in ritual for the purposes of libation, other practitioners use sparkling cider or other non-alcoholic beverages: this is particularly true if there are under-aged children in the group. The Wiccan faith system promotes walking a life of balance; a practitioner cannot achieve this through excessive drug or alcohol use. When performing Magick, the practitioner should not use alcohol or drugs. When working with Magick, the practitioner requires a clear mind and the ability to focus. The Wiccan faith system also promotes the responsibility of the self, and while one's sexual practices are private, Wiccans do not in any way encourage or promote risky or abusive sexual behavior.

MYTH: Wiccans have rituals in secret because they are doing things that they need to hide.

TRUTH: *Wiccan rites are sacred and therefore kept private.*

This does not mean that practitioners are doing shameful things or that they feel that they must hide their actions because they are doing something wrong. Wiccans have rituals in private, not because they have things to hide, but because they do not want others who do not understand or appreciate their practices to taint the atmosphere they are trying to create in ritual. In contrast, sometimes Wiccans welcome respectful non-practitioners into open circles so they can witness special rites of passage.

MYTH: **The Bible says that practicing Magick is sinful; this means Witches are evil.**

TRUTH: *Wiccans are not Christians. They do not rely on the Bible as a religious text.*

There is no arguing the fact that the Bible indicates that the practices of Witchcraft are an abomination. While some people choose to base their life on what the teachings of the Bible offer in a literal sense; other people have the free will to follow what is true for them in terms of religious practices and understandings. True Wiccans are not evil or sinister, but this will not stop certain individuals from believing that they are, despite any arguments to the contrary. For those who follow the Bible, there are many indications alerting followers to refrain from practicing Magick because it is believed to take powers that are attributed to being part of "God's domain." For the sake of argument, if it is one's soul-felt belief that the Bible is their guide and they must live their life accordingly, and if that person believes Magickal practices are spiritually and morally wrong, the solution is simple: Do not practice Magick, but leave others to make their own decisions about what is spiritually appropriate.

MYTH: **Satan deceives Wiccan practitioners into believing they are following a legitimate religion when they are really worshipping him.**

TRUTH: *Wiccans do not believe in the Judeo-Christian Satan or the devil and therefore do not consider themselves deceived by a non-existent, evil being.*

Wiccans have found a personal truth that allows them to evolve spiritually and to worship a God and Goddess. Due to the disbelief in Satan or the devil, some people believe that Wiccans are individuals that Satan has misled into worshipping him in the guise of a "benign deity." What's more, because some individuals believe that Satan has misled Wiccans, they also maintain the belief that anyone who chooses to participate in Wicca and its practices are in league with the devil. Unfortunately, it may be that there is no convincing

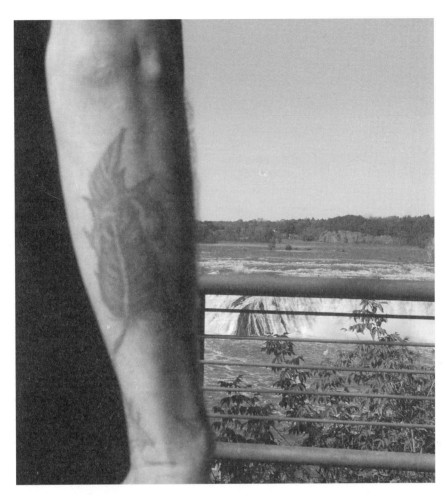

Tattoo of a feather symbolizing the element of air. *Courtesy of Justyn Staley.*

such individuals otherwise; people that believe Wiccans have been deceived by the devil will often attribute Satan and his power to all personal views on the matter. Bear in mind Wiccans don't believe in a devil that holds dominion over all things but it does not mean that they do not believe that evil exists. Wiccans believe in the polarity of all things. In order for good to exist, evil must also exist.

MYTH: **Witches have tattoos that symbolize the devil's mark.**
TRUTH: *Tattoos are not "devil's marks," or "Witches marks."*

In the past, a person accused of Witchcraft would have endured a bodily search for a mole, birthmark, wart, or other

Tattoo of the Green Man: a representation of the Masculine Divine. *Courtesy of Justyn Staley.*

Tattoo of a triquetra, fire, and vines: a symbol of the Divine Trinity, the element of fire, and the element of earth. *Courtesy of Justyn Staley.*

bodily defect believed to be indicative of a pact made with the devil; hence, the notion of a "devil's mark."[29] Of course, the presence of bodily markings or tattoos have nothing to do with evil or Satan. Biblical teachings, in Leviticus 19:28, forbid tattooing: "Ye shall not make any cuttings in your flesh for the dead, nor print any marks upon you: I am the Lord."[30] The latter verse explains why tattooing is viewed as something sinful by some individuals. Tattooing, in Wiccan circles, is perfectly acceptable and is nothing more than a meaningful form of art. Some Wiccans like having tattoos, others don't; sometimes the tattoos have a religious significance or may signify a rite of passage, and sometimes they do not, but at no time do they have anything to do with representing devil worship.

MYTH: **To become a Witch, the individual renounces his or her former religion, and pledges allegiance to Satan.**

TRUTH: *Wiccans do not believe in a devil. A person converting to Wicca renounces their former belief system by letting go of their previous beliefs to adopt the understandings of a new religion.*

As you can see, this myth is only partially true. First, since Wiccans do not believe in a devil, a person does not swear allegiance to Satan when becoming a Witch. No one baptizes the individual in Satan's name if the individual desires to convert from one faith to another. Wiccan dedications and initiations differ from one tradition to another and from Christian rites. A person converting to Wicca renounces their former belief system by letting go of their previous beliefs to adopt the understandings of a new religion. The act of renouncing one's religion does not involve the defilement or intentional disrespect of the individual's former religious affiliations. While the practitioner is walking away from their former religious path, they are taking on a new belief system absent of any allegiance to Satan.

MYTH: **Samhain or Halloween is the devil's holiday.**

TRUTH: *Samhain (pronounced Sow-en) or Halloween, is not the devil's holiday.*

Wiccans celebrate, honor, and remember their ancestors and all those who have passed before them on Samhain. Samhain is similar to Memorial Day; Wiccans remember loved ones and ancestors on the high holy day. It is a marker of the time when light has passed into darkness (late fall to early winter). In the past, since winters were difficult and food scarce, the time often brought tests and harsh trials. Wiccans associate the holiday with the dead because of the "seasonal death," people witness in nature. There is nothing evil about Samhain or practices occurring during the day's festivities. More about Samhain and Wiccan holidays is available in Chapter 3 of this text.

MYTH: If you decide to leave the Wiccan faith, there are special measures you must implement to do so.

TRUTH: *If someone decides to leave the Wiccan faith behind, when ready, he or she can make the decision to do so.*

While one must dedicate oneself to The Craft and its practices when becoming Wiccan, leaving The Craft is quite simple. There are no rules one has to follow before leaving, and no one forces a person to remain a practitioner. There are no repercussions for choosing another spiritual path.

MYTH: If you become Wiccan, you are defying God and you will go to hell.

TRUTH: *Wiccans do not believe in the existence of hell.*

Some Wiccans believe stories pertaining to hell stem from actual physical places in the world, but Wiccans do not believe in a physical hell where people suffer for their sins. Most Wiccans believe in karmic repercussions, in reincarnation, and some practitioners believe in the Summerlands: a place where the spirit goes between life incarnations after death. By now, it should be clear to the reader: Wicca and the beliefs within the faith system are not inherently evil.

MYTH: Wiccans do not believe in Jesus Christ or God.

TRUTH: *Wiccans do not worship the God as described in Judeo/Christian/ Muslim religions, and they do not worship Jesus.*

Paradoxically, Wiccans argue, "All Gods are One God." Some Wiccans do not believe that Jesus Christ existed at all, while other Wiccans believe that Jesus existed, but that he is not the Divine savior. Instead of considering Jesus as a Divine being, sometimes people view Jesus as a mortal man or a prophet who recognized the Divine within and who tapped into the natural power of healing and Magick in order to help others, just as Witches do.

MYTH: Wicca is a self-centered religion.

TRUTH: *The Wiccan religion is not about ego; Witches see the Divine in themselves and in others, but they also see themselves as an integral part of the universe.*

Some people might interpret such an understanding as being a concept in a "self-centered religion," but this is not to say Wiccans are, by nature, conceited or they participate in a religion with a sole focus on the self. Wiccans are definitely all about soul-awareness, world-awareness, and personal growth. They seek to be an integral, active part of the world and to make a difference; this is far from the common actions one would identify with a self-centered individual or a person who participates in a religion that promotes egocentric behaviors.

MYTH: Wiccans revere nothing.

TRUTH: *Wiccans honor all of nature, worship the Old Gods, and hold the respect for the Divine and nature above all else.*

Wiccans not only revere all of life, they believe life is a sacred gift. They revere the earth, its bounty, all creatures, the Divine, and the Divine within every individual.

MYTH: Wiccans don't believe in sin, so it allows them to get away with whatever they feel like doing.

TRUTH: *Despite the disbelief in the concept of sin, it does not mean Wiccans have no beliefs that help shape their moral decisions.*

Wiccans do not believe in the concept of sin and do not use the concept to define moral behaviors. However, many Wiccans believe in karma and the repercussions of one's actions: The belief in karma serves as a moral compass, a guide, or a measure in order to keep one's actions ethical and positive.

MYTH: Wiccans require God's salvation and one should lead them to the Christian path: the one true faith.

TRUTH: *Suggesting that a Wiccan needs to be saved crosses some serious personal boundaries.*

Witches follow centuries-old religious traditions, and they do not want anyone attempting to convert them. If a Witch ever decides the Wiccan religion is not the right spiritual path, the individual is free to leave and convert to another religion. Witches find the Wiccan religion and its principles spiritually fulfilling. They ask of others tolerance so that they can engage in their religion without criticism or questioning. They do not attempt to proselytize, and they appreciate the same courtesy from others.

MYTH: **It's okay to tell a Wiccan, "I will pray for your salvation."**

TRUTH: *Telling a Wiccan practitioner you are going to pray for his or her salvation clearly implies the Wiccan's religious practices and beliefs are misguided.*

Wiccans are not seeking salvation let alone something that can only be acquired through someone else's prayers. Wiccans do not find that prayers for salvation are necessary at all. To imply Wiccans need salvation is to suggest that Wiccans are on the wrong spiritual path. It's is discourteous to do so, and no one has the right to decide for another individual what is right for one's spiritual well-being. Witches honor everyone's right to believe as one chooses and expect the same tolerance.

MYTH: **Wiccans are materialists, overly concerned with personal prosperity, and are in no way spiritual.**

TRUTH: *How much Wiccans crave material goods and prosperity will vary from one individual to the next.*

In Wicca, a significant emphasis on spirituality exists, and a concentration on the material world is solely up to the individual. The Wiccan tenets do not promote a focus on acquiring material items; rather, the tenets of the faith promote balance, integrity, and honor in all things. Wiccans are discouraged from using Magick for the sole purpose of personal gain, and they are encouraged to use the Magickal Arts in wholly positive ways.

MYTH: **Wiccans use Magick because they want to control others or to gain power.**

TRUTH: *Ethical Wiccans believe in protecting the free will of the self and others. They therefore do not use Magick in an effort to control people.*

Wiccans are interested in Magick as a technique for healing, spiritual evolution, and self-improvement. A responsible practitioner does not decide to study and practice the Magickal Arts because he or she desires power. Rather, a practitioner enters into the study of Magick for the purposes of learning how to improve one's life, the lives of others, and how to intensify one's connection with the universe and the Divine. The practice of Magickal undertakings involves the understanding that free will must always remain intact and an excessive desire for power only leads to ruin.

Myth: **Wiccans are anti-Christian.**
Truth: *There is no inherent dogma of animosity in the Wiccan faith.*

Wiccans are not Christians and have a different set of views and practices. Even today some Wiccans struggle with the invalidating and discriminating attitudes of others, some of whom are Christians, and therefore arguments and resentments can and do occur. There may be some parts of the Wiccan community that, in a backlash against judgments and rude remarks, distance themselves from or react strongly to members of the Christian community who openly judge, denounce, or criticize Wiccan beliefs. There have also been centuries of oppression including and following the Witch Craze of Medieval Europe, otherwise known as the Burning Times, which lends to religious tensions between members of different faiths. Wiccans do not follow the teachings of Jesus, but they are not necessarily "anti-Jesus." Wiccans believe each person has a path to follow, having a different path is acceptable, and they respect the rights of individuals to follow their beliefs. Practitioners of the Wiccan faith appreciate the same tolerance in return. Just because Wiccans see things differently does not mean they are evil or anti-Christian; it just means they are different, and having different beliefs from another group or religious organization does not make Wiccans "anti" anything.

CHAPTER 2

MISUNDERSTOOD PRACTICES
AND HISTORICAL MISCONCEPTIONS

"We must forever confront
intolerance and Witch hunts
with integrity, clear vision, and courage."
~Danvers Preservation Commission
1992

Many Wiccan beliefs and practices remain misunderstood by non-Wiccans and neophytes (or novice) in The Craft. Witches must strive to correctly inform others about basic Wiccan practices and beliefs. Accurately sharing one's knowledge of the faith system is the first step toward promoting religious tolerance. More importantly, neophyte Wiccans desiring to learn the fundamentals of the faith system should do so with a profound and unwavering sense of integrity.

Wicca is a flexible religious system. There is no single way to learn about the tenets of the faith or the Magickal Arts. Since there are so many ways of learning and practicing The Craft, neophytes must take great care in selecting educational resources and teachers. Solitary practitioners are in danger of becoming lost on the path of learning, especially if the practitioner lacks the support of one or more Pagans who can guide them along their path. This does not mean a solitary practitioner cannot master an understanding of Wicca and Magick without help, but the learning process is easier when someone has knowledgeable, experienced, and scrupulous practitioners to lend educational and spiritual support. Wiccans participating in covens are also potentially in danger of being misguided as they advance in their learning if they become members of a less than reputable coven. Thus, it is paramount when choosing educational resources and teachers, whether a solitary or a coven member, that practitioners do so with considerable care.

There are neophyte Wiccans lacking the basic understanding of what the religious holidays represent, when and why tools are used in The Craft, and some even lack the basic understandings necessary to keep psychically and physically protected when working with Magick. For neophyte practitioners, an unclear understanding of Magickal principles and Wiccan philosophy, at minimum, can diminish the power and significance of one's spiritual and esoteric experiences. In a worst case scenario, using Magick incorrectly can result in "the dabbling effect" where the practitioner endures the repercussions stemming from chaotic, abusive, or the erroneous use of Magick. In addition, in order to promote religious tolerance, practitioners must possess a solid understanding of the Wiccan faith and the principles shaping all Magickal and religious undertakings. After all, it is impossible to help others to understand what the Wiccan faith offers to its practitioners if one does not hold a firm understanding of what makes the religion and its practices meaningful and spiritually fulfilling.

MISUNDERSTOOD PRACTICES

MYTH: **You are only a true Witch if you are a hereditary Witch.**
TRUTH: *While there are hereditary Witches, being born into a family of Witches is not a prerequisite for being a Witch or a Wiccan.*

A hereditary Witch may gain the advantage derived from a Witchly lineage where practices are handed down from one generation to the next, but this does not mean that being born into a family of Witches is the only way to become a Witch. Many people are the first in their family to embrace the Wiccan faith. Being the first Witch in a family does not make a practitioner any less of a real Witch just because practices were not handed down from an earlier generation. A non-generational Witch has to learn The Craft and Wiccan tenets by either finding a reputable teacher or through solitary studies. The process involves self-motivated learning, and the non-generational Witch may lack some of the resources that a generational Witch has at his or her disposal. But this does not prohibit the future success in the individual's practice.

Whether a generational or non-generational Witch, when a practitioner has children, the Witch may not always pass down their beliefs or share their traditions with their descendants. Some Witches prefer to allow their children space to explore other beliefs until they are ready to choose their religious path.

Inevitably, Wiccan parents are bound to influence the learning of their children as they model their religious values and priorities, even if they do not intentionally share their beliefs or traditions. However, being born into a Wiccan household is no guarantee an individual will become an adult with Wiccan-based religious preferences. Thus, some Witches are hereditary Witches and some are not; having familial roots consisting of people involved in Witchcraft is not a Magickal or religious *proviso*, and the absence of a Witchly lineage does not diminish one's potential or capacity for being a Witch.

MYTH: Anyone can be a Witch by stating he or she is a Witch.
TRUTH: *There are no "Witch police" to stop people from calling themselves whatever they want, whether the person earns the title or not. However, an individual has to do more than call him or herself a Witch in order to be a true practitioner.*

To be a Witch involves a lifetime of study, learning, and applying knowledge with wisdom and reverence. Just as the act of dabbling in Witchcraft does not make a person a Witch, stating that one is a Witch and not backing it up with the practices and lifestyle of a Witch does not make a person a Witch.

MYTH: Wiccans have no Bible; therefore, they have no religious literature.
TRUTH: *Wiccan tenets come from a variety of literature and organizations.*

As the sacred text of the Judeo-Christian faith, The Holy Bible consists of a combination of instruction, ethics, and prayers believed to be the literal or symbolic word of God, depending on the follower's faith. This text does not contain elements of the Wiccan faith. Wiccan beliefs stem from ancient Pagan practices. No matter how Divinely inspired a particular work may be, there is no single sacred text in

Wicca. There is a book entitled, *A Witches' Bible: The Complete Witches' Handbook* by Janet and Stewart Farrar, but not every Wiccan reads or relies on this particular book for religious instruction. Wiccan tenets come from a variety of literature and organizations. Witches also have grimoires (sometimes identified as a *Book of Shadows (BOS)*: books containing rituals, spells, and other Magickal information, and some maintain a Book of Mirrors where they document their Magickal experiences. However, the latter books are not bibles. In essence, Wiccans consider all knowledge sacred and derive their religious understandings and tenets from a variety of sources.

MYTH: **Wiccans have no set of governing spiritual laws to adhere to and they do whatever they want to do.**

TRUTH: *Wiccans do have a set of governing spiritual laws based upon common sense, ethical behavior, and attempt to align behaviors and actions with the "An if it harm none, do what you will" rule.*

Of course, "will" does not equate to whatever one "wants." Wiccan spiritual laws are just as rigid, if not more so than the tenets of other religions, only they are more simple in terms of expression. Practitioners try to protect their spiritual karma, to adhere to the Rule of Three, to adhere to tenets expressed in the *Principles of Belief,* and the *Witches Rede of Chivalry* on a daily basis. Wiccans also adhere to the *Thirteen Goals of a Witch* as they strive to spiritually progress throughout their lives. Responsible Wiccans have the ethic of "harming none," governing their actions. They use Magick to heal, and to bring about positive changes in their lives. They have a serious respect and reverence for nature that governs their choices to treat Mother Earth with respect. In addition, responsible Wiccans are mindful of the free will of others and do not seek to control or manipulate those around them.

MYTH: **Wiccans are idolaters and they revere graven images.**

TRUTH: *Wiccans believe in a Goddess and a God who have a multitude of aspects, names, and characteristics. Wiccans don't worship graven images; they worship what the images represent.*

The God and Goddess, when unified, make up one Divine being. Wiccans work with and revere different aspects of the Divine so that the Divine can be more easily understood. The forms of the God and the Goddess are throughout all of nature as well as in the human mind. Art often personifies abstract concepts.

Goddess candle: a representation of the Feminine Divine.

Witches use statues, images, and representations of the Goddess and God as a way of helping to visualize the Divine, but they do not pay reverence to the physical images or statues. Instead, Wiccans honor what such things spiritually represent. In Judeo-Christian religious understandings, the use of such statues and images does indeed make Witches idolaters. According to Judeo-Christian teachings, the Gods and Goddesses that Wiccans worship are false Gods. To Wiccans, there is nothing "false" about the deities they revere and honor; Wiccans perceive and pay reverence to the Divine in a different way than people practicing monotheistic religions, and their deities are just as valid as any other concept of the Divine. In addition, there are some people practicing monotheistic religions who use statues in worshipping the Judeo-Christian God, in worshipping Jesus Christ, or in paying homage to the Virgin Mary. Doing so is no different from when Wiccans use statues or images to help personify the God and Goddess. Outside the practices of a religion, this is similar to American showing patriotism by saluting the flag, and treating the symbol with respect; it is not a reverence for the flag, it is a reverence for what the symbol means.

MYTH: Wiccans follow a religion stressing moral autonomy; the tenets of the religion are lenient, and they promote indulgence.

TRUTH: *The tenets of Wicca are not lenient, and they do not promote indulgence.*

As it is with any religion, the individual ultimately defines what beliefs and morals he or she will adhere to; even belief systems heavily riddled with tenets do not necessarily define how a person will behave in every situation.

Free will is an element influencing how every person will act. The apparent flexibility of the Wiccan religion is something people are often attracted to, but the faith system is not as flexible as it might appear. While Wicca offers a great deal of personal choice, there are rules and guidelines that Wiccans should follow, however, the degree to which a Wiccan adheres to the tenets of the faith is based on the individual's understanding of the principles, one's free will, intent, and moral compass. As in all belief systems, a religious person may or may not adhere to the tenets of a religion in every situation or at all, but just because a person decides to behave in a way that is not aligned with one's religious beliefs, doesn't mean that the faith system promotes unethical or indulgent behavior.

MYTH: Wicca borrows precepts from the Christian bible.
TRUTH: *Wicca is a faith system based on ancient Pagan practices, and such practices are not derived from the Christian bible.*

Our faith system is rich, deep, and complex. It may appear as if some of the tenets of Wicca stem from the bible, especially due to the commonalities between Wiccan and positive Christian tenets, but many Christian understandings are adaptations of Pagan beliefs. As mentioned previously, during the rise of Christianity, Christians adopted and transmogrified Pagan holidays, traditions, and beliefs in order to make Pagan to Christian conversions more palatable for Pagans.

MYTH: Wiccans solely focus on revering a Goddess; the God is not emphasized and is undervalued.
TRUTH: *This is not an inherent part of the Wiccan faith, but the idea resonates with many practitioners who feel they have been seeking the Goddess in a culture that often does not readily recognize and neglects the Feminine Divine.*

A stark contrast to well-known monotheistic religions with the focus on a single, male God form is the prominence of Goddess worship in Wicca. The Goddess is not only the mother of all, but Her status is equal to the God's, if not greater in some cases. The image of the Goddess as Maiden, Mother, and Crone also creates an image of Her power, and it sometimes implies She is more significant than Her consort, the Father, Son, and Sage or the God. There are some traditions placing full focus on the Divine Feminine and some groups do not permit men in their circles.

In contrast, many Wiccans believe in the duality of all things and they pay reverence to both the Masculine and Feminine Divine. Due to the suppression of women in other patriarchal religions, Wiccans emphasize the feminine aspects of the Divine in order to counteract such oppression. Some non-Wiccans and neophyte practitioners may confuse the emphasis of the Feminine Divine with a de-emphasis on the God or Masculine Divine in Wiccan practices; thus, Wicca is sometimes erroneously considered a "Women Only Religion," "Feminist Religion," or "Goddess Religion." Emphasis on the Goddess in the Wiccan faith is a re-emergence of the Feminine Divine; it is not a counter attack or hostile response to the emphasis on the single, masculine God of monotheistic religions or the Masculine Divine in the Wiccan faith.

Some practitioners, like Dianic Wiccans, whose primary deity is the Roman Goddess Diana, often emphasize the Goddess over the God. Some Dianic Wiccans only worship the Goddess. The emphasis on the Feminine Divine attracts a number of followers who seek to balance the matriarchal/patriarchal scales by apparently tipping them to the other extreme. A tendency to draw attention to the Goddess is present because for many, God as Divine male is *status quo* and has been the norm in religion for centuries. Emphasizing

The Goddess Diana and the Stag King.

The Earth Goddess.

the Divine Feminine seems to hold the attention of those who have sought it; suddenly a balance in the spiritual void is realized when one no longer follows religious systems de-emphasizing, ignoring, or excluding a Feminine Divine aspect. The emphasis on the Feminine Divine is not an absolute, nor is it a tendency in all Wiccan practices. In the most basic sense, Wicca is about balance and this includes a balance between masculine and feminine energies. The Hermetic axiom "As above, so below," becomes an ideal in which the Divine Masculine and Feminine are also held in balance.

MYTH: **Wiccans worship trees.**
TRUTH: *Wiccans honor plants, rocks, the water, the sky, the earth, animals, people, and all of nature: They hold these things sacred.*

Wiccans honor nature, but this does not mean Wiccans worship trees; they recognize the sacred Divine in all things. Practitioners may also embrace the teachings about the Tree of Life, a concept in the Cabbala as well as other religious teachings suggesting the interconnectedness of all things in the universe, the mirroring qualities of the microcosm and the macrocosm, and how the Divine courses through all things.

MYTH: Tarot cards are evil and their use attracts evil spirits.
TRUTH: *Tarot cards, which are pieces of card stock with symbolic pictures on them, are not inherently evil.*

There are many different types of Tarot decks, and while their symbolism and artwork may vary from one deck to another, Tarot cards are not negative. The idea Tarot cards are evil comes from the belief that using any form of divination goes against the laws established by God. Tarot cards are a divination tool used by the reader as a guide to point out upcoming obstacles and challenges. The cards, designed in Renaissance Italy, incorporate major Judeo-Christian and Pagan symbols and themes. When messages are delivered through Tarot cards, the reader is tapping into the higher consciousness or the Divine (depending upon individual belief) for life guidance. The messages the cards offer are not set in stone, and the cards can be used as a decision making guides since they offer information about what might happen if the reader remains on a certain course of action. Tarot cards can also give insight on how a person can make positive changes in their life. Meanwhile, the "Death" card is not always indicative of a pending death, and the card is primarily a symbol of change, and the "Devil" card is not about the devil, rather it is about the reader's excessive focus on the material plane, or it can represent an intense connection with creative forces. The media misuses the Death card and the Devil card often; this has also led to confusion about the nature the Tarot and its use.

MYTH: Wiccans use the female form or another human body as an altar.
TRUTH: *Some Wiccans allow a person to act as an altar, but the majority of practitioners rely on altars constructed out of a variety of materials.*

They may place altars inside or out, and an altar might be a table made of oak, glass, or it can be something outside like a large tree stump, an outdoor table, or a large, flat rock. Some altars are round, some are square, and some are small dressers or end tables. An altar's size depends on what is convenient in terms of spatial needs. Some practitioners prefer to break down their altars after every Magickal working and some Witches leave their altars set up at all times. Altars are sacred and serve as a storage area for Magickal tools, as a location for Magickal workings, and as the practitioner's center of worship. Some practitioners might allow a female to act as an altar during a sacred rite, but this is not true in many cases.

One of many different ritual altars.

Another altar style.

A serpentine athame and an Isis athame.

MYTH: Witches use an athame to cut people or animals during their rites.

TRUTH: *An athame can be sharp, but it does not have to be since it is not for cutting anything in the physical.*

An athame is a ritual blade used to assist in visualizations and to help aim visualized energies in the direction the practitioner wants it to go. Sometimes a practitioner uses an athame to cast a Magick circle or to cut a doorway while in circle. The creation of a doorway allows a Witch to enter and exit a circle without having to release it and start the circle-casting process over again. An athame can be sharp, but it does not have to be since it is not for cutting anything in the physical. In fact, if a Witch exposes an athame to any blood, the tool is no longer good for ritual purposes.

MYTH: Magickal tools are always necessary. For example, a practitioner cannot construct a Magick circle without an athame, sword, staff, or wand.

TRUTH: *A Witch can cast a circle with nothing more than their intent and visualization abilities.*

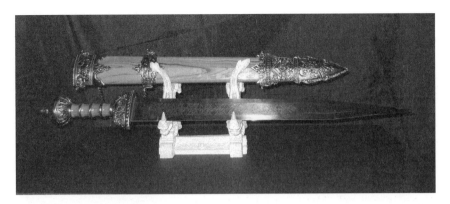

A Roman sword used in ritual.

A practitioner uses an athame, a double-edged ritual knife, to direct energies. Practitioners can also use a sword, a wand, or a staff to cast as circle, whether store bought or handmade. However, in the absence of flashy tools, a Witch can still construct a circle. A Witch can cast a circle with nothing more than their intent and visualization abilities. Magickal tools are great and useful accessories, but in a pinch, a practitioner can do without tools; Magick comes from within and the will and intent of the practitioner serves as the power behind one's Magick. The chief tool of the Witch is the self. In essence, tools are cool, but the Witch's mind and will rules.

MYTH: Practicing Wicca requires a person to have a large income so that he or she can afford expensive tools.

TRUTH: *If this were true, there would be few Wiccans, and they would all be wealthy.*

Advancement in Wicca and one's spiritual evolution does not relate to the depth of one's purse. Wiccan beliefs do not require any type of tithing, monetary sacrifice, or payout to any governing board or system. If a specific coven or working group has administrative fees or fees associated with running their religious organization, they can seek donations or fees that are sometimes eligible for tax-exempt status. As far as the independent study and practice of Wicca, like most things, it can be as expensive or inexpensive as one chooses. Specialized schools of Wicca and associations exist which benefit from the donation of their patrons, but it is not essential to attend such schools or to belong to specific associations in order to be a Witch and practice the Magickal Arts.

Beautiful jewelry, elaborate costumes, or custom-made ritual tools can be wonderful additions to a Wiccan's Magickal inventory, but are not necessary. The library offers books about the Magickal Arts, so many books can be accessed for free. It helps to have paper and pens to take notes or to record rituals in a ***Book of Shadows***, but when all else fails, an individual can get inexpensive supplies or they can be made from household objects. In times of extreme financial difficulty, the practitioner desiring expensive tools can wait until his or her financial situation improves.

When performing a ritual, the concept of "offerings" is included to express gratitude to the God and Goddess for the many blessings one receives. These offerings are sometimes coins, even pennies, tobacco, or stones, but may also be feathers, herbs, or things found in nature. A practitioner can find fancy tools in unusual places and through various means. A coauthor of this work obtained a beautiful cauldron when a loved one found the large and lovely antique and exchanged landscaping services for the tool. If a person is meant to have a certain tool or object, the universe will find a way to unite that person with it. In the meantime, if one's ritual chalice is a simple drinking glass, it is perfectly acceptable providing one treats the tool with the respect that any Magickal tool deserves by using it solely for Magickal purposes.

MYTH: Wiccans wear the symbol of the devil, a pentagram, and consider it a form of Magickal protection.

TRUTH: *A common myth results in the misuse and misunderstanding of the terms pentacle and pentagram. Wiccans do not wear a symbol of the devil.*

Technically, a pentagram is a five-pointed star with a single point in the ascendant. The Wiccan symbol of protection, the pentacle, is often confused with the symbol of Satanism, a inverted pentagram. A pentagram enclosed in a circle can be either a pentacle or an inverted pentagram, depending upon the positioning of the star inside the circle. Once, both the pentacle and the inverted pentagram had positive connotations, but eventually, the inverted pentagram took on a negative meaning, particularly when it became a symbol of Satanic worship. Some Wiccans view the inverted pentagram as a symbol of higher Magick, but many Wiccans refrain from wearing the inverted pentagram at all because of the negative connotations presently associated with the symbol.

The pentacle: a star enclosed in a circle with one point facing upward. *Image made with elements from Anita Lee Creations.*

A pentacle has one point facing upward, while a pentagram has two points facing upwards. The pentacle is a symbol that represents the four cardinal directions: air, fire, water, and earth. The upper point represents Akasha: the combination of all of the elements. The circle of the pentacle also represents the neverending cycle of birth, life, death, and rebirth since many Wiccans believe in reincarnation. The points also represent the seasons of the year: spring, summer, autumn, winter, and the top point represents spirit or the Divine.

The Pythagoreans saw the pentagram as a symbol of perfection.[1] Early Christians viewed the *pentangle* as a symbol of the five wounds of Christ, the five human senses, the five virtues of knighthood, and the five joys of the Virgin Mary.[2] Later, Heinrich Cornelius Agrippa, a renowned magician, mathematician, astrologer, alchemist, and occult writer wrote about pentacles; he depicts the pentagram enclosed in a circle with a single point facing upward as well as inverted pentagrams in his writings. Like the Pythagoreans, Agrippa assigns the pentacle with the numerological association of the number five, explains the number five has "great command over evil spirits," and, he asserts *pentangles*, having five points, can be used to "drive away devils and to expel poisons."[3] Agrippa's understanding of the pentagram still associated the symbol with positive meanings.

In the nineteenth century, however, Éliphas Lévi, an occult author and magician,

The pentagram: a star enclosed in a circle with two points facing upward. *Image made with elements from Anita Lee Creations.*

associates the pentagram with the Goat God Baphomet. Some references suggest Baphomet was originally revered by the Knights Templar and that Lévi's nineteenth century portrayal of Baphomet is the same deity. During the Inquisition, many of the Knights Templar were tortured and executed. While being tortured, some confessed to honoring a being called Baphomet. It is possible that such confessions were false and that there really was no reverence of Baphomet at the time. Thus, to suggest that the pentagram took on negative connotations during the Inquisition is likely a spurious argument. In *Dogme et Rituel de la Haute Magie* (*Dogma and Ritual of High Magic*), Lévi explains the pentacle, when inverted, represents evil, and the symbol attracts negative forces. Lévi writes:

The pentagram with two points in the ascendant represents Satan as the goat of the Sabbath . . . The pentagram is the figure of the human body, having the four limbs, and a single point representing the head. A human figure, head downwards, naturally represents a demon; that is, intellectual subversion, disorder, or madness.[4]

The Goat God Baphomet; sometimes the head of Baphomet is superimposed over the image of a pentagram.

Later, in the twentieth century, the Church of Satan adopted the symbol of Baphomet superimposed over a pentagram as its symbol. When portrayed in such a way, the two points of the pentagram facing upward comes to represent the God's horns. It also came to represent the opening of the gates of hell in order to draw up hellish or chaotic energies or it symbolically represents the release of hell on earth. The pentagram then becomes a symbol representing the perversion of the concept of spirit prevailing over mundane desires.

Sometimes, in Wiccan circles, the inverted pentagram comes to represent an initiate's established connection with the elements, but this is not always the case. What's more, some practitioner's of Ceremonial Magick perform the Lesser Banishing Ritual of the Pentagram: a ritual used to cleanse an area in preparation for a ritual. To complicate the matter further, the media and Hollywood often interchange the pentacle and the inverted pentagram and this confuses people about what the symbols mean.

Today, many but not all Wiccans refrain from wearing the inverted pentagram despite the earlier positive connotations associated with the ancient symbol of protection. The inverted pentagram has dual connotations for the Magickal community, and it is up to the individual to discern what the pentagram conveys. Nevertheless, practitioners must remember that non-Wiccans, unfamiliar with the history of symbolism associated with the pentacle or pentagram, will often see either symbol and perceive it as indicative of devil worship.

MYTH: **The pentacle and the Star of David are the same symbol.**
TRUTH: *Many people confuse the Star of David with the pentacle. The Star of David is a six-pointed star and the pentacle is a five-pointed star; the symbolic meaning differs.*

The Star of David is a hexagram with six points, and it is made of two intersecting triangles: one pointed upward and the other down. The Star of David, otherwise known as the Magen David, is a star found in the Cabbala, and is a symbol often used as a protective Magickal amulet.[5] It looks similar to the Seal of Solomon, but the latter symbol has additional features thereby making it different from the Magen David Star.

MYTH: **Satanists and Wiccans follow the same law: Do what thou wilt.**
TRUTH: *The Satanic law is "Do what thou wilt." The Wiccan law is "do what you will, harm none."*

The Satanic law is a system based on exploiting the basic desires and urges of the ego, promotion of the self, and one's own goals to the exclusion, or sometimes even to the detriment, of others. The Wiccan law is "do what you will, harm none," and it implies one's spiritual and life path is open for exploration as long as, in doing so, the individual does not seek to violate the rights of or bring harm to others. It is the practitioner's responsibility to align his or her practices so that they serve the greater good of the situation or community. It does not mean a person has free reign to do whatever they please. A clear distinction exists between the two laws. The law Wiccans follow asserts that one must consider the consequences of one's actions before taking action. Wiccans therefore must consider all actions and the potential karmic repercussions. They must also reflect on how their actions will affect others.

MYTH: **The Horned God that Wiccans worship is Satan.**
TRUTH: *The Horned God that Wiccans worship is The Stag King, Pan, or Cernunnos, not Satan.*

Sometimes Wiccans identify with the God as The Green Man. Early Christians, when attempting to convert Pagans, equated the

Stag horns representing the Stag King.

The Greenman; Lord of the Woodlands.

Pagan Horn God with Satan. Doing so made it easier to demonize the Horned God and what the God represents. The Horned God of Paganism emerged from the earliest religions in prehistoric times. As a nature God sometimes portrayed with horns (sometimes horns and hooves), he is a protector of the forest and things dwelling within it. He represents fertility and abundance.

Ancient cultures revered the Horned God, especially throughout Pagan Europe. Later, the Horned God became the Goddess's consort, the deity who brings fertility to the Mother Goddess.

Even later, with the prevalence of European monotheistic views and successful campaigns establishing dominion over Pagan cultures, people began viewing the fertility-based Horned God as a symbolic representation of something that was dirty, shameful, and evil. It seemed only fitting to the evolving culture where views differed greatly regarding sex and procreation, that a deity portrayed as part animal and associated with sex and fertility must have some perverse and impure agenda. This translated to the newer, comparatively more recent, belief in the devil. The adapted understanding resulted in the transition from the life giving, virile Horned God of animals and nature, to the lusty, deceitful, animalistic figure of the devil.

Myth: Wiccans, Satanists: it's all the same thing.
Truth: *Wiccans and Satanists are two distinct groups of people with different beliefs.*

People have dragged the word *Witch* through theological mud for centuries. At best, people often perceive the term *Witch* as describing an evil seductress or the word defines any of the dangerous aspects of femininity. At worst, the same term describes a consort or servant of the devil. To confuse matters more, as mentioned previously, female practitioners of Satanism sometimes call themselves Witches too.

Wiccans view the confusion between Satanists and Wiccans as an insult and vice versa. Wiccans and Satanists are two distinct groups of people with different beliefs. Satanists are, for the most part, anti-Christian; this idea stems from the Hebrew translation of Satan meaning the "adversary of man and God"; thus, in paying reverence to the devil, Satanists are clearly illustrating anti-Christian sentiments.[6] In some instances, Satanists profess not to really care about Christian ideologies or about purposefully inverting Christian rites/symbols, and the "reverence" paid to Satan is more an act of mocking the dogmatic teachings of the church. Meanwhile, the chief problem many Wiccans have with Christianity is the assertion by some of its followers that Christianity is the only path of truth. Wiccans also do not mock other religious systems in practices or rituals, and they do not use inverted symbols from other faiths.

Wiccans have no belief in the devil since it is a Judeo/Christian/ Muslim concept. Some Satanists call upon or invoke demons in their rituals, while this is not the case with Wiccan rituals or practices. Satanists also partake of a religion with a large focus on the self: one that is materialistic and about one's personal pleasure and gain. Satanists might even use Magickal practices in an effort to harm others or in an effort to control others as only one law is followed, "Do what thou wilt." In contrast, the chief tenet of Wicca promotes the idea of following one's will while simultaneously ensuring to "harm none," in the process.

Wiccans have reverence for the earth mother and all of life. They use their knowledge to heal, to help others, and they understand the intricate connection of all human beings and creatures. The beliefs Wiccans adhere to stem from the indigenous practices of those who lived closely connected to the earth: systems of belief far predating monotheistic religions such as Christianity. Hence, the belief in or the worship of any devil or Satan is irrelevant when it comes to Wicca, for Satan is a Judeo-Christian construct and plays no part in the earlier religions predating monotheistic religions.

A further point of confusion among non-Wiccans arises from the century's old practice of a newer, dominating culture vilifying the symbols, beliefs, deities, and understandings of the previously indigenous culture. For example, the early European settlers saw Native Americans as "savages," who worked evil and who needed to be "civilized;" this belief prevailed well into the twentieth century. Likewise, when the British colonized parts of Africa and dominated various regions, they saw the natives and their religious beliefs in the same manner. A close examination of history will reveal this same pattern of the follower of new religions demonizing the deities of the old religions repeatedly. When Judeo-Christian beliefs gained in acceptance and became an institutionalized part of Western culture, often the previous Gods and Goddesses and their attributes became synonymous with evil. For instance, Poseidon's pitchfork is now the tool of Satan. Further, the God of the forest, Pan, depicted with horns and hooves, becomes synonymous with Satan after the vilification of Pagan concepts by dominating religions.

Distortions about Witchcraft continually arose throughout history and further added to widely held misconceptions about Witches. Ironically, misconceptions about The Craft were often times a byproduct of sociopolitical agendas and had little to do with religion or morality. There are more proclamations of Witchcraft being the work of the devil when social and political unrest yield the need for a scapegoat. In times of peace and prosperity, society tends to tolerate Witches, seek them out for their unique skills, or ignore them altogether.

To be perfectly clear: Wiccans have nothing to do with the devil, directly or indirectly. They do not engage in Satanic worship at any time. Just as there are people who will refuse to recognize

Wicca as a valid religion, there are people in society who will insist that Wiccans worship Satan, despite what arguments are set forth explaining otherwise. Any true Wiccan will denounce the false and erroneous belief that Wiccans are devil worshippers. No Wiccan would intentionally make the Satan any part of their practice.

MYTH: Witches draw evil spirits because of their practices.
TRUTH: *The intent and disciplined mindset of the practitioner dictates what energy is drawn to him or her and the type of Magick that is practiced.*

Some people assume that Witchcraft and Magickal workings will attract evil, wreak spiritual havoc in the practitioner's life, and stir up trouble for whomever the practitioner encounters; this is not the case. Like attracts like: If someone has their mind focused on negative and evil, then it is more likely a person will attract evil. Dabbling in Magick without proper knowledge of the arts may attract undesirable negative energy, but this does not mean Witches intentionally draw negative spirits to them. Since the Wiccan faith involves life affirming beliefs and rites, such practices have nothing to do with attracting evil forces or spirits.

MYTH: Witches can give you lucky charms to bring luck into your life.
TRUTH: *While Witches use various charms and they can offer others charms for prosperity or luck, many Wiccans believe everyone is responsible for bringing positivity into his or her own life.*

There is no Magick more powerful than the kind powered by one's own will and intent. Since many Wiccans believe in the Three-fold Law of Return, the best solution to bring luck and positivity into your life is to lead a fulfilling, positive, and compassionate life. Witches are not here on this planet to solve all the world's ills. If they could do so, they would have done it long before now.

MYTH: A Witch's familiar is a demonic entity that assists the Witch in Black Magick practices.
TRUTH: *A familiar is not a demonic or evil entity; it is an animal sharing a loving, spiritual bond with a Witch.*

In the 1500s and 1600s, it was a common belief that female Witches could shape-shift into different forms, but the most common form cited was that of a black cat.[7] The latter belief went hand-in-hand with the idea that cats steal the breath of babies while they slumber, among other superstitions about cats. Later, the "demonic familiar" was a shape-shifting companion: one of its many guises was that of a black cat; superstitious beliefs held that Witches were also capable of transforming into black cats as well.[8]

Familiars are sometimes black cats, but not always: Any animal a person has an affinity for can be a familiar. Sometime Witches can have more than one. Familiars can be dogs, birds, cats, owls, snakes, and some Wiccans even call upon mythical creatures as familiars.

Familiars have a special bond with their Witch companion. Familiars are able to lend energies when needed; this concept is unique in polytheistic religions and no doubt appears strange and unusual to some. Wiccans acknowledging the existence of evil or "lower level entities" would never seek to bond their animal companions with nasty energies and they would not have any use whatsoever for any animal possessed by evil.

Working with familiars is not required, but it can be a fulfilling and rewarding practice. Familiars can communicate through dreams and meditation and can provide comfort and support in Magickal workings. In addition, for most people who enjoy

Some Witches have dogs as familiars; Precious and Puggles, Dayna's familiars.

Many Witches have cat familiars. Clyde, Justyn Staley's familiar.

Morgan La Gray, Angela Kaufman's familiar.

Isis, Patricia's familiar.

Zephyrus, Angela's second familiar.

Brigid, Justyn Staley's second familiar.

the company of animals, sharing one's life with a familiar brings a multitude of rewards, even on a mundane level. Familiars do not need to be cats, or even house pets, but it is helpful to have a close bond and regular contact with them. There is nothing negative in the bond between a familiar and a Witch. Any notions of sacrifice, cutting, mutilating, or any other concept related to familiars or related to any part of Wicca is the product of much misinformation and fear. Witches often believe animals choose to be familiars and consent to assist the Witch in Magickal workings.

When working with a familiar, a Witch does not drain an animal of their vital life force. When done correctly, this practice is a unifying experience between the energy field of the human and the animal. The connection between the familiar and the Witch lends direction and intellectual focus to the instinct and natural drive of the animal. The Witch also benefits from the energies the animal lends as well as the affectionate bond developed between the animal and the practitioner.

MYTH: **Some Wiccans practice White Magick and some practice Black Magick.**

TRUTH: *The practitioner's intent defines magickal practices and outcomes.*

Even in the non-Magickal community, people recognize Black Magick as a source of evil. It involves the intentional use of the Magickal Arts to harm others or to control another's free will. Black Magick is a form of self-serving or cursing Magick associated with unethical practitioners and Satanists, and it is even falsely associated with Wiccan practitioners on occasion. White Magick includes practices involving healing, benevolent blessings, and Magick used for the attainment of positive goals; some Wiccans only practice White Magick. Meanwhile, Gray Magick involves the use of Magick for protection, spiritual/psychic self-defense, and for calling upon the forces of justice. Using Gray Magick gives the practitioner the ability to block energies meant to harm and to return the energies to the sender, as well as to invoke energies intended to establish protective barriers when required. Martial Arts teaches that the use of excessive force is unethical and the mastery of martial arts skills are for self defense only; this rule also applies to the use of Gray Magick when defending one's self spiritually and psychically. Some Wiccans practice both White and Gray Magick. The practitioner defines Magickal outcomes; Magick, when used for positive purposes, results in positive outcomes.

MYTH: **Wiccan rituals sometimes involve orgiastic gatherings, and all Wiccans practice ritual in the nude.**

TRUTH: *Some Wiccans practice in the nude or "skyclad" and some do not. Some Wiccans add the practice of Sex Magick in rites, and some do not.*

To do so is to illustrate the freedom from restraints of the mundane world or the concept of sin. Some coven members may find practicing skyclad far too distracting as it may hinder the focus on the ritual working. It is not necessary to perform rites skyclad since Wiccans can express their freedoms using alternative methods. Some practitioners are comfortable with performing rites skyclad and find the experience physically and spiritually liberating. If a practitioner is seeking to join a coven he or she will want to ask the coven members if they perform rites skyclad or not.

In a similar fashion, the use of Sex Magick is a personal choice. While Sex Magick produces powerful energy that practitioners use for Magickal purposes, it is not a necessity, and common sense applies with its use. The use of Sex Magick is something based on the personal preferences of the practitioner, and it's important to realize that most, but not all, who do partake of such practices do so in private as a couple. Practitioners sometimes replicate the union of the God and Goddess in Wiccan rituals, but Witches can also use symbolic representations of such a union, and live demonstrations are not necessary.

MYTH: **All Wiccans practice Sex Magick.**
TRUTH: *Some practitioners use Sex Magick in a ritual to re-enact the Great Rite, but not all covens do.*

When a Wiccan engages in Sex Magick, the working is about the physical/spiritual union of two people, a reenactment of the God and Goddess's union, and the mingling of the two auras of the people creating the sexual energies. The Great Rite is a replication of the union between the God and Goddess often re-enacted on Beltane, one of the eight Witch's holy days. The act of sex is not merely a physical connection; it is a symbolic reference to the birth of the universe and the marriage of the Goddess and Her Consort. In the absence of a sexual act, inserting the athame, a phallic-like Magickal tool, into the chalice serves as a symbolic replication of the Great Rite. In fact, the ritual chalice alone is also a symbolic representation of the joining of the God and Goddess. The chalice's stem is phallic-like and the cup symbolizes the female womb.

It is up to the practitioner to decide if Sex Magick is something that is personally appropriate. Of course, responsible Wiccans do not condone under-aged sex. In addition, Responsible coven leaders or members do not force a coven member to participate in Sex Magick if they are not ready or if they have no desire to do so. Some people are more comfortable refraining from the practice of Sex Magick. For others, sex is a powerful form of energy, and the practice of Sex Magick is therefore perfectly acceptable.

Sex Magick may not be appropriate for a practitioner and a practitioner's partner in every instance. For example, if the Wiccan practitioner is in a relationship with a Christian, the couple might avoid the use of Sex Magick so the beliefs of both parties remain respected. When Sex Magick is used, the participants must be completely comfortable with the act. During a sexual encounter, practitioners raise heightened energies. The sexual energies aid the practitioners in achieving a desired result on the physical plane. There is nothing foul or inappropriate about Sex Magick, and many Wiccans appreciate the beautiful spiritual and physical connections formed between the participants. Bear in mind that the full consent of all parties is necessary; if a party did not consent, it would destroy the positive energies that the act is supposed to manifest.

Sex Magick has nothing to do with having sex with demons, entities, or the devil. Wiccans do not view sex as sinful. While the view of sex is more liberal in the Wiccan faith system than in many other religions, this does not mean Wiccans partake in bizarre sexual practices with supernatural beings.

MYTH: **A Witches' coven must consist of thirteen people or the coven is not completely established.**

TRUTH: *A coven can consist of three or more people and a coven can even have more than thirteen people.*

Some covens decide to "hive off," and the hiving results in clans or groves. The initial coven has an elder who might branch off and start another coven in order to break the larger group into two, but the two covens often remain connected to one another in such an instance. Whether a coven has only a few members or many, the number of members participating in the coven does not reflect the completeness of the coven's formation.

MYTH: **The number thirteen and Friday the 13th are unlucky; covens base their membership on thirteen people because of the negative connotations associated with the number thirteen and as a way to mock Jesus Christ and his disciples.**

TRUTH: *Many people consider the number thirteen unlucky, but this is nothing more than superstition taken to the extreme.*

Many buildings do not have a thirteenth floor, and often house numbers will skip right over the number thirteen. Many people often worry about bad luck and bad things happening on Friday the 13th too; this notion has a number of potential origins and it may be associated with the gospels. Some people believe the crucifixion of Christ occurred on a Friday, and consider the day particularly unlucky if the Friday falls on the thirteenth day of the month: as if one is doubling the potential for ominous events. Some superstitions assert the number thirteen is an allusion to, as well as a mockery of, Christ and his disciples at the Last Supper, and according to Old Norse superstitions, seating more than twelve individuals at any dinner table results in the thirteenth person dying before the year's end.[9] The Norse superstition stems from the idea that Judas was the thirteenth disciple of Christ, and after betraying Jesus, hanged himself.[10] Still, other events shape the notion that Friday the 13th is an ominous day, and the superstition stems from a number of different beliefs throughout history.

Wiccans recognize the number thirteen is a Magickal number. It is the number of moons in the year (although sometimes there are only 12 moons in a year), there are thirteen esbats celebrated each year (if there is a blue moon during the year), and sometimes the number thirteen is the upper limit of membership in a coven. Nevertheless, if there are thirteen people in a Wiccan coven, it has nothing to do with mocking Christian practices. Wiccans do not consider Fridays as an unlucky day; in fact, in ancient times, Fridays are days dedicated to the Goddess of pleasure and love, and in Norse myth, the day receives its name after the Goddess Frigga.[11] Thus, the assumption Wiccans base the upper limits of coven membership on the number thirteen for negative purposes is all together incorrect.

MYTH: **Wiccans conduct rituals, only in the dead of night, while wearing long flowing robes and pointed hats.**
TRUTH: *Wiccans have rituals during the day, at night, and anytime they see fit to do so.*

Wiccans sometimes dress in ritual attire and sometimes they wear casual clothing. Some Witches may enjoy wearing long robes and conical hats, while other Witches are perfectly satisfied in celebrating rituals in dressy clothing they have designated for the specific purpose of ritual use. Meanwhile, only holding ritual "in the dead of night," is not practical. What's more, some Wiccans residing in cities may not have an outdoor area to hold rituals. Although Wiccans follow the tenets of the old ways, they live in a modern world; they add traditions to their practices, and they adapt Magickal rites to suit their unique and busy lifestyles.

MYTH: **Wiccans have rituals where they use blood in their rites. They sacrifice animals and people during rituals or spell workings.**

TRUTH: *There are some covens and solitary practitioners that may use blood in their rites, but many Wiccans do not use blood in ritual or spell workings. At no time is harming an animal or person encouraged or condoned.*

Some Wiccans believe that blood is the essence of the life force, and as such, blood lends powerful energies to Magickal workings. Bear in mind that relatively few Wiccans use blood in their rites. For Wiccans who do not use blood in their rites, they do not drink blood, use blood in spells, and do not use blood to make oaths or pacts. A Wiccan *never* sacrifices animals or people. The whole notion of Witches sacrificing people and using blood in rites originates from the ancient misogynistic beliefs about women. In the *Malleus Maleficarum*, authored in the late 1480s and a work that served as a guide to identifying, questioning, and torturing accused Witches, authors Heinrich Kramer and Jacob Sprenger assert:

> [Witches] kill and eat children, or devote them to the devil if unbaptized. They cause abortion… raise tempests and hail-storms which devastate whole regions; they bring the plagues of locusts and caterpillars which devour the harvests; they render men impotent and women barren, and cause horses to become suddenly mad under their riders. They can make hidden things known and predict the future, bring about love or hatred at will, cause mortal sickness, slay men with lightning, or even with their looks alone, or turn them into beasts.[12]

Cultural and religious shifts resulted in society viewing women as second-class citizens who were evil, seductive, and conniving as parallels were drawn between women and Eve in the biblical creation myth. The notion led to the subsequent belief that all women are easy to persuade so that they will act against the laws imposed by the Judeo-Christian God. Even worse, society deemed women as temptresses, people that could tempt males into straying from the straight and narrow religious path. Later, the notion of the Witch as a vicious, vindictive, seductress bent on performing all acts of evil became a widely held view. In fact, it was believed the more heinous a Witch's acts were, the more evil the Witch and the greater the likelihood that she would merit powers delivered onto her by Satan.

MYTH: Wiccans practice black mass.
TRUTH: *Wiccan rites do not involve mimicking the religious mass of another group, the perversions of sacred objects, or the invocation of evil spirits.*

The rites in Wicca are God and Goddess-oriented and are not parodies; practitioners do not focus on malice toward any group or person, and they do not deconstruct the beliefs of another group. Ultimately, all Wiccan rituals are life affirming and positive. Wiccans do not mock, imitate, or degrade other religions during their rites, and black masses are not part of their practices.

MYTH: Wiccans raise the dead in necromantic rites.
TRUTH: *Most Wiccans believe the spirit world is not beyond the reach of the living, but while communicating with the dead, they do not seek to raise the body of the deceased physically.*

Necromancy is the practice of raising the spirits of the dead and communicating with them for the purposes of divination.[13] More specifically, in the past, sometimes the necromantic arts have been associated with the act of instilling a corpse with temporary life in order to receive information from the deceased about future events.[14] If the latter definition of necromancy is considered, then one can easily argue Wiccans do not practice this form of necromancy; Wiccans *do not* seek out freshly deceased corpses, and they *do not* raise the dead to do their bidding in their rites. Some Wiccans, however, communicate with spirits, spirit guides, and deceased ancestors, and in some cases, Wiccans attempt to help the earth-bound spirits cross over as well.

Most Wiccans believe the spirit world is not beyond the reach of the living. It is common for Wiccans to honor the dead by acknowledging their ancestors and giving honor by memorializing their deceased. On Samhain, in particular, it is a common practice to open one's self up to messages from the dead. The veil between the physical plane and the realm of the deceased is thinnest. For many Wiccans, communication with the dead is an experience that naturally lends itself as an extension of their beliefs; they may still communicate with a deceased loved one through meditation or ritual or may leave a tribute to the deceased in part of their sacred space. Wiccans recognize spirits have their own purpose, and Wiccans do not try to harass or corner the spirits of the dead. Wiccans do not attempt to force the appearance of spirits via provocation so they can appear, perform tricks, or respond to demands. Witches also do not seek to entrap the spirits or hold them hostage for their own purposes. Wiccans give honor and seek to learn from spirits, but they do not seek to force the manifestation of the deceased. They know when a person dies; the spirit has its own work to do, and its own spiritual journey to fulfill. When communicating with spirits, Witches do so with respect and proper protection because not all spirits are what they claim to be. Wiccans also keep in mind the understanding that just because one has passed on, it does not mean a spirit is waiting around for the purposes of communication.

MYTH: **All psychics are Witches.**
TRUTH: *Wiccans believe all people have latent psychic abilities whether they are Witches or not.*

Witches believe in the innate seemingly "supernatural" abilities every individual has: They believe in innate abilities as set forth in the "Thirteen Principles of Belief." Thus, Wiccans do not view psychic abilities as a part of Witchcraft. It is something every person is born with: a birthright. Wiccans enhance and use psychic abilities for positive means, but they also recognize not every individual is in tune with his or her innate abilities. Witches do not consider psychic abilities supernatural, but rather something perfectly natural and a part of being human.

MYTH: **Wiccans dress in dark clothing or they dress in Gothic attire.**
TRUTH: *While it is true many Wiccans wear black attire, it has nothing to do with being Goth or trying to look Gothic. Many Wiccans wear black because they believe the color black serves as a barrier against negative energies.*

Every color has a special vibration and purpose. Wiccans use different colors to help balance their lives. They also utilize colors to control the energies surrounding and influencing them day-to-day.

Some Wiccans may like the Gothic-look, and there is nothing wrong with the preference. Meanwhile, a Wiccan practitioner might refrain from wearing black at all. Often times, teenagers become interested in Wicca and begin wearing black clothing frequently, either because they have come across literature that has explained to them the positive properties of the color or because they like the color. Sometimes teens, in the process of trying to discover who they are, make an effort to stand out from the rest of the crowd by being different and wearing black attire often. There is nothing wrong with doing so as it is perfectly natural for a teenager to explore who they are and to express their individuality. Ultimately, the choice to wear black has nothing to do with being evil, being sinister, or with the reverence of dark forces.

Visually, black is the mixture of all colors. When mixing paints, if combining all of the colors of the color spectrum, then the result is the color black. Symbolically, black retains the power or energies of all colors. Black is also a spectrum of light absent of color. As a wave of light, black absorbs all other colors and the color therefore serves as a protective color by absorbing any negative energies one encounters.

This same view of colors as a visual pigmentation and a visible light wave also explains why Wiccans will visualize white light surrounding them for protection from negative energies as well. In color theory, white is the absence of all color and the color has absorbing properties. As a spectrum of light, white light is the combination of all color frequencies. Akin to white noise, a mixture of all sound frequencies, white light waves have the energies, properties, and frequencies of all colors and therefore offer a barrier of protection from negative energies.

There are other occasions where Wiccans wear attire for specific Magickal purposes; for example, one might wear brown attire to emphasize grounding or blue attire to enhance his or her mood. While some Wiccans may gravitate toward Gothic-style attire, others prefer different styles of clothing. Color has significance in Wiccan practices, but color selection is not the be all and end all to the methods for choosing attire.

MYTH: **Wiccans cast hexes on people.**
TRUTH: *Wiccans do not put hexes or curses on people, places, or things.*

If a person is truly Wiccan and a follower of the path, they must follow the credo: "Do what thou will, harm none." Wiccans believe strongly in the Rule of Three, with the understanding that what they put out into the universe comes back to the practitioner times three. If a practitioner puts forth positive energies then those energies will return, multiplied, onto the practitioner. If the practitioner puts out negative energies, then negative energies return to the practitioner multiplied. Wiccans believe in karmic laws where holding them cosmically responsible for all of their actions, whether they are positive or negative. In essence, if Witches were to cast hexes and curses on people, those energies would come back upon the practitioners in a negative manner.

Let's face it; everyone gets angry from time to time and Witches are just as capable of becoming irate as anyone else. As Witches however, practitioners strive to find ethical means of resolving conflicts that model the "harm none" philosophy. A Wiccan does not use Magick to harm. Magick is an art form that practitioners use for the purposes of self-defense, but one should not wield it as a weapon. Wiccans are more likely to seek a positive resolution to their conflict. Magickally trampling upon others or attempting to hurt them is not the typical resolution a Witch seeks. The teachings of Wicca ethically prohibit a Witch from using the knowledge of Magick to curse, hex, manipulate, or harm anyone in anyway. It is against the Wiccan code of ethics to infringe upon the free will of another. Thus, no one who is a true Wiccan will perform curses or hexes of any kind.

Love spells are not a good method for finding genuine love.

MYTH: All Witches cast love spells if you ask them too.
TRUTH: *There are Witches who will cast loves spells upon request, free or for a fee. However, many Wiccans feel it is highly inappropriate to cast a love spell for one's self or for anyone else.*

Love spells can cause havoc and many Wiccans believe that when casting love spells it takes away or affects a person's free will. Wiccans frown upon any effort to influence the free will of others. What's more, when casting a love spell to make someone fall in love, if the spell works and the practitioner gets what he or she desires, then the practitioner might wind up with more than originally expected, and could wind up with someone who becomes obsessed with him or her. Using love spells, in some instances, is like making use of a "build-your-own-stalker kit." Further, the type of love one receives because of a love spell is not real love at all. It is the practitioner's influence over someone else's free will. This makes the casting of love spells aimed at specific people senseless.

As mentioned earlier, Wiccans are aware of the forces of karma, and of the importance of not infringing on the free will of others. If adhering to the latter guidelines of Wicca with a solid, grounded sense of ethics would not use love spells. Nevertheless, one can find some love spell kits in stores and online. If seeking real love in a loving relationship, love spells are not the answer. There are however, "love spells" used to draw love into one's life in a general sense that do not involve altering the free will of another person. It is okay to cast a spell where one attempts to bring love into one's life, provided one retain respect for the free will of others and the practitioner does not purposefully attempt to make a specific person fall in love with someone.

MYTH: Witches can perform Christian exorcisms, if you ask them, to in order to alleviate paranormal activity.
TRUTH: *Witches do not perform Christian exorcisms.*

An Christian exorcist performs the *Rituale Romanum* or Roman Ritual consisting of litanies, psalm recitations, prayers, commands, and other various measures to exorcise evil spirits or demons. Church officials must first deem such actions necessary. Meanwhile, some priests, church representatives, or lay demonologists will conduct Christian exorcisms without seeking the approval of the church. Witches do perform house blessings, clearings, cleansings, or banishing (equivalent to a Christian exorcism) in order to exorcise evil spirits or "lower level entities." Wiccans adapt rituals to suit particular situations, and they sometimes perform crossing ceremonies for spirits in addition to banishings and house blessings.

MYTH: **All Wiccans use Ouija boards and have séances to communicate with spirits.**

TRUTH: *While many Wiccans are capable of using Ouija boards (pronounced Wee-jah) and conduct séances for communication, it does not mean they all do.*

Wiccans use psychic communication as well as other means of spirit communication. Many Wiccans recognize the spirit world to be as valid as the physical world. In this case, it would be as natural to communicate with spirits, as it is to interact with the living. The means of such interaction may vary.

There are many methods for communicating with spirits far less dangerous than holding séances or using Ouija boards. Sometimes Wiccans or people in general communicate with spirits via psychic abilities or they use scientific methods of investigating spirits and

A Ouija Board often used for the purposes of spirit communication; however, it is not a recommended practice.

communicate with spirits through electronic voice phenomena. Ouija boards are dangerous, both physically and psychologically. At minimum, a person does not know who or what they are really communicating with when they use the Ouija board or when they call on spirits in séances. Some people manipulate Ouija boards and events during séances; therefore, a person cannot be sure of the validity of any communication one might experience. In a worst-case scenario, a person can end up connecting with something he or she might not want to connect with and the individual may find it difficult to break the connection or get rid of it after making contact.

As Wiccans and paranormal investigators, the authors of this text have investigated a number of paranormal cases where clients have used the Ouija board in order to communicate with spirits to find out the source of paranormal activity, and in the majority of cases, the use of an Ouija Board only served to aggravate the situation further. While there are some suggested safe methods for the use of the Ouija, when in doubt, it is best not to do anything at all and to leave the Ouija Board out of any efforts to make a connection or to communicate with any spirit. The authors of this text do not promote the use of Ouija Boards or séances since the use of such practices can lead to spirit intrusion, infestation, manifestation, possession, misfortune, and a whole host of baneful consequences associated with what negative entities can and do impart.

MYTH: **Wiccans cast spells and this makes them evil.**
TRUTH: *Spell casting does not make Witches evil; and Wiccans do not put hexes or curses on people, places, animals, or things.*

This idea is a misconception stemming from a centuries old belief that only a monotheistic God has the authority to create one's life circumstances, and to take the initiative to harness the powerful forces of Magick to create change is much like "playing God." Some people argue the Bible defines Witchcraft is evil, so being a Witch and spell casting is evil. In such cases, as unfortunate as it may be, no amount of debate will change the mind of individuals convinced of the evils of Witchcraft. Wiccans do not adhere to the Christian Bible, even if some of the precepts in the New Testament illustrate a loose resemblance to Wiccan tenets. Meanwhile, additional fears about Witches and spell casting arise when people fear the use of Magick to cause them misfortune.

Wiccans do not practice spells to cause harm, and a spell is only as good or as bad as the practitioner's intent behind the spell working. Responsible Wiccans strictly adhere to the Wiccan Rede. In some ways, the power of prayer and the power that supports a spell working are similar. For example, imagine if someone were to light a candle and incense as an offering to the Goddess or God, and then he or she lit a bundle of sage and walked around their home in a clockwise or deosil direction while asking the Divine to cleanse, bless, and protect their home. The latter spell is a positive working or a cleansing. Spells involve the use of carefully chosen words and meaningful objects, and spells are sometimes performed on specific days, hours, or under certain planetary influences in order to express and intensify one's will and intent. Spell working is about bringing one's intent or thoughts into manifestation in positive ways.

Myth: All Wiccans are either vegans or vegetarians.

Truth: *As a matter of survival, people must eat; as Wiccans, personal preferences define what a person eats and how one feels about consuming particular food sources.*

Stating "all Wiccans" conform to one specific practice is as much a stretch as stating "all Jews," "all Christians," or "all Buddhists," subscribe to a set pattern of behaviors found in every member within a described group. This practice of generalization does disservice to the potential understanding and acceptance of the diversity that can help us celebrate individuality. Rather than assuming all members of a group act a certain way, it is wiser to appreciate the differences among people even within the same religious groupings.

Some Wiccans are vegans, some Wiccans are vegetarians, and some Wiccans eat meat. Some Wiccans hunt and see the use of an animal without waste as acceptable. Some Wiccans are meat eaters and find it difficult to give up the love of a tasty cheeseburger every now and again! Alternatively, some Wiccans may view the act of eating meat in direct violation of the rule Wiccans adhere to: "An it harm none, do what you will," and they feel it is a natural part of their reverence for nature and animals to refrain from eating meat. Meanwhile, other Wiccans have no problem with consuming meat, and believe applying the "harm none," rule to dietary practices is somewhat nonsensical because it can also be said plants are being harmed during the process of consumption.

Some Wiccans might refrain from consuming meat in order to make a statement about not being in support of corporate or abusive farming practices. Some Wiccans make dietary choices based on their health needs; for example, a person might refrain from consuming dairy due to lactose intolerance or another Wiccan might not eat a certain food because of allergies. As a matter of survival, people must eat; as Wiccans, personal preferences define what a person eats and how one feels about consuming particular food sources. Many Wiccans will give thanks to the animal or plants for their sacrifice before consuming the foods they eat. Some Wiccans also bless or consecrate the foods they eat before consuming them.

HISTORICAL MISCONCEPTIONS

MYTH: Witches are not real. They are merely characters in stories; they are green, fly on brooms, and eat bad little children.

TRUTH: *Witches are not only real, they are nothing like what is depicted in fairy tales.*

They are not the fairy tale version of Witches so many people read about as children. Witches do not boil unbaptized children to make flying ointments; they do not stalk little children who have lost their way in the woods and stuff them into a raging hot oven when they desire an evening snack, and yes, in the real world, Witches have families, jobs, and responsibilities. There were many extreme, stereotypes perpetuated during the Medieval Witch craze for political purposes, and such stereotypes are false. Witches are everyday people with a different religious and world view.

MYTH: The United States government does not recognize Wicca as a valid religion.

TRUTH: *Although it took many years, the United States government recognizes Wiccan traditions on a state and federal level.*

A number of different court cases assert the protections of Wiccan practices. Witches have rights protected by The First Amendment in The United States Constitution which supports the right for all people, including Wiccans, to believe as they choose and to practice their religion: "Congress shall make no law respecting an establishment of religion, or prohibiting the free exercise thereof. . . ."[15] Thus, a person has the right to choose and practice a religion without the law interfering with one's right to do so, providing one adheres to the existing laws of society.

The Green witch of fairy tales; not at all a depiction of the modern day Witch.

At first glance, the First Amendment suggests the government is not in a position to "recognize," any religion at all. According to Dana D. Eilers, a well-known Pagan author and attorney who has written a comprehensive legal treatise on the rights of Pagans in America, "Wicca is a religion meritorious of First Amendment protection."[16] The constitutional law chapter of her book, "Pagans and the Law: Understand Your Rights," addresses this topic in depth. On the issue of whether Wicca is "recognized" by the United States government, Dana asserts:

> Theoretically, the United States government should not be in the business of "recognizing" religions as this would be a violation of the Establishment clause of the First Amendment. However, from a practical standpoint, the United States government is absolutely in the business of determining which spiritual practices rise to the level of religions and which of them will be "recognized" because the IRS grants tax exemptions to churches and religions all the time. Additionally, certain religions are permitted their symbols on the graves of veterans in VA cemeteries and some are not. Therefore, one can make the argument that the United States government goes about recognizing religions and certainly, Wicca is among those recognized." *

* Eilers, Dana D. "Re: Question on the U.S. Government's Recognition of Wicca." Email to the author. August 7, 2010.

Many state and federal level cases have played a role in making Wicca a religion the government recognizes. In addition, within the *Religious Requirements and Practices of Certain Selected Groups: A Handbook for Chaplains*, the government recognizes Wicca as a valid religion.[17] The United States Army still uses the pamphlet to ready chaplains for helping others with a variety of spiritual beliefs, including Wicca. Later, the 1980s case of *Dettmer v. Landon* resulted in Judge John D. Butzner, Jr., of the United States Court of Appeals for the Fourth Circuit in Virginia, concurring with the United States District Court, ruling that Wicca is a legitimate religion and not an assortment of disparate occult practices.[18] Many other cases exist establishing the legal recognition of Wicca; for more information, examine Dana D. Eilers's book: *Pagans and the Law: Understand Your Rights*.

Today, when it comes to changing laws and the social views of Wicca as a bona fide religion, Wiccans are making headway, but progress is slow. Even as Wiccans make small steps toward greater religious tolerance, challenges still exist.

In recent years, after much debate, the Department of Veterans Affairs agreed to allow the addition of pentacles, as a religious symbol, on veteran headstones. Later, in 2010, an Air Force academy in Colorado established an outdoor circle of stones for Pagan gatherings and worship; but someone desecrated the site with a makeshift crucifix, and similar events have occurred at other established centers for Pagan worship.[19] Wiccans do not find Christian symbols offensive, but when someone places such symbols on Pagan centers of worship, it is no different from having someone spray paint a pentagram on a church wall: It is a clear, deliberate act conveying religious intolerance.

Wicca is a legitimate religion from an objective and legal standpoint; however, there are still people who refuse to accept Wicca as a recognized religion. Likewise, there are people who reject certain scientific theories, refuse to acknowledge the rights of homosexuals, or the "realness" of things perceived as "outside of the norm." Wiccan beliefs do not fit into the rigid religious concepts some people hold; there will always be members of society that reject Wicca as a valid religion. In some cases, no amount of arguing will change certain opinions about Wicca and its legitimacy. The bottom line is this: Many members of society recognize Wicca as a valid religion, and the government recognizes Wicca on a state and federal level. Make no mistake about it: Despite the continued challenges Wiccans face in the effort to defeat religious intolerance, they have legal protections under the Constitution, the right of religious freedom applies to all Wiccans and Witches, and the religion is as valid as Buddhism, Catholicism, Judaism, Taoism, or any other religion.

MYTH: **In 1692, in Salem, Massachusetts, it was a common practice to burn witches at the stake.**

TRUTH: *The people killed during the Salem Witch trials were not Witches.*

If anyone was involved in pagan practices at the time, it was most likely Samuel Paris's servant Tituba. Tituba was severely mistreated, but she was not put to death. The accused Witches in Salem stood out more as political enemies, disruptive neighbors, or those who rubbed local authority or members of the community the wrong way. In America, individuals accused of witchcraft were not burned at the stake. In 1692, following allegations of witchcraft, those in authority hanged the accused. Following his refusal to confess to witchcraft, Giles Corey was pressed to death. Many others were imprisoned. In contrast, individuals accused of witchcraft during the earlier witch-hunts in Europe were burned and tortured by various means.

MYTH: The Salem Witch Trials occurred in modern-day Salem, Massachusetts.

TRUTH: *Although many people believe the Salem Witch Trials occurred in Salem, Massachusetts, they did not and accused Witches were not burned at the stake.*

The actual trials occurred in Salem Village. The area, later chartered into a town, is now Danvers, Massachusetts.

MYTH: The Witch-hunts have ended.

TRUTH: *Recent headlines indicate people are still enduring violent acts or dying following accusations of Witchcraft.*

Many people falsely assume the witch-hunts have ended. While the tragic Witch-hunts occurring in Europe and Early America are long over, Witch-hunts are still happening in the present decade. Today's Witch-hunts still involve individuals who are not even Witches, but are people accused of Witchcraft nonetheless. Real Witches sometimes face similar situations. It is common for some Witches to experience problems with neighbors, on the job issues, and modern-day Witches sometimes face myriad forms of discrimination. Sometimes choosing the lifestyle of a Witch jeopardizes familial relationships and friendships as well. Even if Witch-hunts are not prevalent in Western society, they are still happening and incidents are on the rapid rise in other parts of the world.

Recent headlines indicate people are still enduring violent acts or dying following accusations of Witchcraft. In an article appearing on News24.com, a community in South Africa demanded the resignation of a school principal after he criticized the community for burning homes down during a Witch-hunt.[20] In the Khaleej Times, a similar case appears; in Dubai, when a psychiatrist made claims about using wholly positive energies in order to remedy family disagreements, it resulted in his arrest.[21] People still face the threat of arrest, persecution, and losing their jobs and homes because of Witchcraft allegations. Some people are also losing their lives as they are dragged from their homes, beaten, burned, stoned, imprisoned, or stabbed to death with spears after Witchcraft allegations. Even children do not escape Witchcraft allegations, particularly in regions of Africa where the belief in Witchcraft is widespread. An Internet search for the term Witchcraft in relation to recent news reveals headline after headline relaying similar events. It is clear, after considering such events, that the Witch-hunts have not ended.

CHAPTER 3

WHAT WICCANS DO

"We can choose to function at a lower level of awareness and simply exist, caring for our possessions, eating, drinking, sleeping and managing in the world as pawns of the elements, or we can soar to new and higher levels of awareness allowing ourselves to transcend our environment and literally create a world of our own — a world of real magic."

~Wayne W. Dyer, *Real Magic*

NOW THAT THE BASIC MISCONCEPTIONS about Witches, Wiccans, and Pagan terminology have been addressed, the reader will hopefully have a solid understanding about Wicca and its practitioners. The following section will continue to illustrate realistic Wiccan traditions and beliefs along with their religious meaning. Many people are surprised when they discover that what Witches do is far from the scary, troubling, or intimidating practices portrayed in stereotypical, media-based images.

THE BASICS OF RITUAL

Wiccans have regular rituals, on esbats and sabbats, and sometimes on power days or for other special purposes. A ritual *never* involves a sacrifice of any kind. During a rite, practitioners pay homage to one or more aspects of the Feminine and Masculine

A gypsy pot, a candle, a chalice, an Egyptian statue, and crystals: some tools used in The Craft.

Divine, and Witches take several steps to complete each ritual working.

While examining a general description about what takes place in a ritual, bear in mind not all practitioners have the same ritual format. Any practitioner desiring to participate in a coven working should ask questions about the coven's practices before making a decision to become a member. While exploring basic components of a ritual, and the reason for a rite's performance, also keep in mind, there are few "hard and fast" rules about how to perform rituals.

A statue of the Goddess Isis.

Most rites involve a period of preparation. In terms of preparation, practitioners will often turn their attention to themselves first. The practitioner often cleanses the body before participating in a ritual, and he or she may ground or meditate alone or with coven members before the ritual begins. Some practitioners choose to fast in order to purify the body. Some Witches will also ground and center before a ritual; grounding involves the use of visualization wherein the practitioner releases negative energies into the earth and then draws up positive energies from it. Meditating calms the mind so the practitioner can prepare for ritual. A practitioner uses meditation to set aside mundane thoughts so that only the highest, purest, most positive energies serve as a foundation for ritual workings.

After a practitioner prepares the self via purification processes, he or she purifies the ritual area. The area for the rite can be indoors or outdoors, depending upon the weather and location, and the practitioner cleanses and blesses the area. The cleansing of the area allows for the banishment of any negative energy that may affect the positive energies desired. When working with tools and correspondences, the solitary Witch or one or more coven members will ensure all the tools for the rite are easily accessible. Tools may include, but are not limited to, things like an altar, bells, incense, censors, Magick wands, swords, athames, statues of deities, and things to represent the elements of air, fire, water, and earth. Correspondences, sometimes called Magickal correspondences, are specific tools or actions that will help enhance the mindset of the practitioner during the ritual working. For instance, during a ritual the practitioner's altar cloth, candles, incense, and decorations match colors or themes of the season or themes associated with the purpose of the ritual working.

Some covens have an entry rite in which the individual requests permission to enter into the chosen sacred area for ritual. Some covens may practice an entry rite before circle casting, others may practice it after, and still others may not practice an entry rite at all. When requesting entry, the practitioner asserts his or her intent to pay honor to the ancient deities.

There are many methods for circle casting. The act of casting a circle differs from one coven to another. Solitary practitioners may also develop a preference for a particular circle casting method. In general, a practitioner casts a Magick circle before ritual workings in order to keep negative energies from entering the circle and to create a separation between the mundane and esoteric or astral planes. A typical circle casting will involve the use of Magickal tools (although tools are optional), calling upon the guardians of one's choosing for protection, and visualizing the creation of the Magick circle as the circle casting is performed.

After the circle casting, the practitioner expresses ritual intent. The expression of ritual intent asserts the purpose of the ritual: This may involve the recitation of short or lengthy passages that define the reason for the ritual and the desired outcome of the rite. An invocation of the God and Goddess follows the expression of ritual intent. An invocation involves the act of calling upon the deities chosen for a specified purpose like protection, blessings, guidance, or inspiration. Sometimes after the invocation, practitioners will restate their ritual intentions in order to strengthen the power of the rite. The practitioner then raises energy to empower Magickal workings often follow. Witches raise energies by chanting, drumming, dancing, or other methods.

In some cases, practitioners experience a period of ritual ecstasy after raising energies and invoking the God and Goddess. Ritual ecstasy involves communing with the Divine and feeling a deep connection with the God and Goddess. Ritual ecstasy, sometimes

A drum, a Native American rattle, and a wand.

called spiritual ecstasy, is a form of "ecstatic communion" or trance where the practitioner temporarily becomes one with the Divine, communicates with his or her chosen deity, and draws intuitive understandings from the experience.[1] The transitory experience may last several moments or longer, and allows practitioner(s) to experience an altered state of consciousness. Many practitioners seek the peace, tranquility, insight, and temporary euphoria accompanying the experience.

Following a period of ritual ecstasy (if experienced), is a period where the energy raised, having reached their highest vibrations, will be used by some practitioners to perform spells, divination work, or works focusing on healing and protection. After Magickal workings, practitioners often partake of libation, where all have a little bit of food and drink (the type of food and drink will vary depending upon preference and tradition). Practitioners make a toast to the Divine, to the ancestors, and give thanks for blessings. Practitioners also leave part of the libation outdoors or on the altar as an offering to Gods. When the ritual working concludes, practitioners thank the guardians for their assistance and release the circle.

SABBATS: WICCAN HOLY DAYS

Sabbats are primary holidays celebrated by Wiccans throughout the year. Wiccans have eight sabbats, four of which are greater and four lesser: The assignment of the term lesser does not diminish the significance of the sabbat, but instead signifies that the lesser sabbat is not one of the four Fire Festivals and its dating stems from astrological occurrences that cause the dates for lesser sabbats to change each year according to astrological events. Celebratory practices may vary from one tradition to the next, and the dates of sabbats will differ depending upon the hemisphere where the practitioner resides.

SAMHAIN

ALTERNATIVE IDENTIFICATIONS
Halloween, Summer's End, Last Harvest

NORTHERN HEMISPHERE
October 31 & November 1

Witches' Wheel of the Year.

SOUTHERN HEMISPHERE
April 30 & May 1

SABBAT TYPE
Greater

Religious Meaning: Samhain is the Wiccan New Year. In accordance with observation of the natural cycles, ancient Pagans noted that the darkness of late fall and early winter marked a crossing point between the abundance of summer and the harshness of the dark winter season. The animals slaughtered in ancient times around Samhain would become the sustaining source of nourishment through the harsh winter. The date aligned with the timing between Fall Equinox and Winter Solstice, making it a cross quarter day. It is a gateway between the seasons of light and the seasons of darkness. It was natural to associate the dark, cold, barrenness of winter with death, reflection, hibernation, and struggle; so, Samhain involves paying honor to the dead, the reflection on mortality, and the knowledge of harsh tests to come.

Spiritually, this holiday is associated with death in its deified form, the Crone aspect of the Goddess. The Crone is ancient and holds much wisdom from her long journey. The Goddess is the Guardian of Death and the Afterlife, so this holiday is the practitioners celebration of her power as the season of death arrives. Witches honor The Crone in the way one would honor an elder or grandparent. Practitioners do not look upon the Crone aspect of the Goddess with dread, but do not take Her lightly. By celebrating, Samhain, Wiccans recognize life is a neverending cycle and that one will eventually experience another chapter in their life journey when becoming elders. Honoring the Crone is a Wiccan's way of recognizing the mortality of human beings and that every human being will one day face the final mystery, death. Wiccans believe that after death, rebirth awaits. The perception of death is that it is a gift. It is a necessary transition in one's spiritual path. Thus, Samhain is a reminder that even in death all life is renewed.

As a gateway time or "between time," Samhain is the day the veil between the worlds disappears and access to the spirit world is easiest. Rituals mark the New Year, as Witches have finished celebrating the abundance of harvest and look to starting the goals of the coming season anew. Scarcity may no longer be the reality today, but contemplation and honoring of the deceased, as well as the use of divination to prepare for the journey ahead remain typical practices on Samhain.

Where appropriate, sometimes practitioners light bonfires and offerings are often left for both the deceased and Divine. Sometimes practitioners will light candles to mark the path of those who have passed on. Witches decorate the altar with symbolic décor like jack-o'-lanterns, pinecones, colorful leaves, and seasonally colored (yellow, orange, brown, black, or red) candles.

YULE

ALTERNATIVE IDENTIFICATIONS
Midwinter

NORTHERN HEMISPHERE
December 20, 21, 22, or 23

SOUTHERN HEMISPHERE
June 20, 21, 22, or 23

SABBAT TYPE
Lesser

Religious Meaning: Yule marks the day of the Winter Solstice: the first day of winter. Due to the nature of the relationship between the earth and sun, this day is the shortest in the northern hemisphere and the night is the longest. This sabbat marks the exact opposite of the seasonal height of growth: Summer Solstice. This is the deepest, darkest of winter nights when ancient Pagans sought to kindle hope as they gathered around bonfires, sharing warmth with loved ones and eagerly awaiting the symbolic birth of the Sun God: the child of the Goddess and God. In fact, many ancient cultures consider the height of winter as an event aligned with the birth of a solar deity. It is no surprise then that even in Christian teachings one finds the birth of the savior to coincide with the winter season. It seems the sun is synonymous with hope, and Pagans view the sun God as representing this hope being born anew, restarting the growth cycle.

Yule is the holiday practitioners recognize the symbolic battle of the Holly King and the Oak King: a battle representing the struggle between the forces of youth and stagnation or light and dark. The Holly King represents the dark half of the year, darkness, the waning season, and he symbolically loses His power on Yule, as Yule is the gateway between the light and darkness; the holiday's arrival therefore harkens the approaching light. The Oak King is associated with the strength and light of youth, and His power begins on Yule and waxes until Summer Solstice when He battles the Holly King again and is defeated. It is important to note these aspects are both a part of the same solar deity: They are dual aspects of the same God, and their symbolic representation not only denotes the battle between light and dark, but also demonstrate the different spiritual drives in humankind, and the growing and eventually waning forces of life.

The birth of the Oak King reminds Witches that life does not end with death, but all that lives and what inevitably dies will be born anew to carry on a future journey in some other form. Science supports this idea since energy never ceases to exist; instead, it is in a constant state of transformation. Yule is a holiday of hope and a reminder that the longer, lighter days of spring will soon arrive. Traditions include decorating Evergreens: symbolic due to their strength to withstand winter and representative of the Tree of Life. Additional traditions include wreath making, gift sharing, hanging mistletoe (a symbol of the Holly King), and the making and lighting (or rekindling) of the Yule log. Practitioners sometimes perform spells for peace, general attraction of love, and attracting balance and harmony to one's life at this time.

CANDLEMAS

ALTERNATIVE IDENTIFICATIONS
Imbolg, Oimelc

NORTHERN HEMISPHERE
February 1 & 2

SOUTHERN HEMISPHERE
August 1 & 2

SABBAT TYPE
Greater

Religious Meaning: Candlemas marks the cross quarter day between Yule and Spring Equinox. It marks the early transition of winter to the spring season. The religious significance of this sabbat and its symbolic meaning mimic patterns in nature; just as all plant and animal life is reawakening from slumber, so too are the ambitions of humankind, seeking to align themselves with the growth and fertility of things to come. Early rejuvenation occurs, and

Wiccans see this time of year as the time when the Maiden aspect of the Goddess is coming into power. This is the time of youthful energies, growth, for formulating plans and goals, and for exploring new possibilities.

The energies of the deities in the form of youthful new beginnings surround all things. Wiccans celebrate the earliest stirrings of spring at this time; traditions include dedication and initiation rites since spring is the season of new beginnings, but these rites of passage can occur at any time during the year. Rituals and spells involving new beginnings, goal setting, fertility, and future prospects are common as well. People living close to the land would recognize this as the period when animals are beginning to give milk, and so the emphasis is on nurturing of things both spiritual and mundane. Other traditions include making crafts, candles, making Brigid's Crosses in honor of the Goddess Brigid, and making corn dollies. This sabbat is often marked as a fire festival and the fires of inspiration show modern Wiccans the way to achieve their goals in the coming season. Candlemas is also a fine time for restocking a Witch's cabinet with necessary herbs and tools too.

SPRING EQUINOX

ALTERNATIVE IDENTIFICATIONS
Ostara, Vernal Equinox

NORTHERN HEMISPHERE
March 20, 21, 22, or 23

SOUTHERN HEMISPHERE
September 20, 21, 22, or 23

SABBAT TYPE
Lesser

Religious Meaning: Equinox, as the name suggests, refers to the point in the relationship between the Earth and sun when daylight and nighttime are of equal length. This phenomenon occurs twice a year, at spring and fall. The Spring Equinox is the climax between the early markers of the season with Candlemas and the final passage from spring to summer with the arrival of Beltane. At Equinox, the journey of the Sun God has progressed from birth (Yule) to childhood and youthful exuberance (Candlemas) and now is approaching a new level of maturity. Likewise, the Goddess in Her many aspects is developing from early youth to maidenhood and the spring season is marked by reminders of the courtship between the God who will soon represent fertility, and the Goddess of nature.

At this time, the earth reawakens and in aligning with these energies, Wiccans seek to invoke enthusiasm for new projects and goals, and to bring to life motivating energies. Equinox is both physically and symbolically a holiday celebrating balance. It is a point where the light and growth promoting forces of nature are equal to the nocturnal, "darker" forces. The darkness associated with winter, the Crone, or death, and the light associated with growth, hope, and the Mother aspect of the Goddess are in full reign. The Goddess and God, in their youthful guises, hold equal power over nature. They will soon join forces to bring in the bountiful growth season. This sabbat reminds a practitioner that, throughout many cycles, there comes a point of balance, and no condition in nature remains in a single state with any amount of permanence.

During Spring Equinox Wiccans celebrate the beginning of spring; pastel and flowery colors are appropriate for this season and traditions include painting or coloring eggs, since they are associated with the new period of fertility. Wiccans may choose this time of year to perform spells to attract fertility in both a literal and symbolic sense. This is traditionally a time of spring-cleaning (the transition from dark to light coincides well with taking an inventory of what one can let go of and what the practitioner wants to hold on to in his or her life). Witches decorate the altar and sacred temple with lovely spring flowers as well.

BELTANE

ALTERNATIVE IDENTIFICATIONS
Beltane, May Day

NORTHERN HEMISPHERE
May 1 & 2

SOUTHERN HEMISPHERE
October 31 & November 1

SABBAT TYPE
Greater

Religious Meaning: Beltane is another cross quarter day between Spring Equinox and Summer Solstice. Beltane marks the climax of the spring season, as it will soon give way to summer. On this day, Wiccans recognize the Goddess and God are awakening all of nature. At this time, the desires for growth and regeneration in the spiritual and physical are also awakened in the practitioner. Ancient Pagans witnessed the heightened fertility of animals and nature at this time of year, and saw the "spring fever" as reflecting the drive within Divine forces to merge and procreate. The Divine union between the God and Goddess then, would bring about the combination of masculine and feminine energies necessary to promote life in all its forms in the universe. This holiday then becomes a time of acknowledging the sacred regenerative forces in nature as humans depended on the growth and fertility of animals and plants for survival. Even today, Wiccans have an inner desire to develop a balance between the masculine and Feminine Divine energies.

Whether the sexual aspects of this fertility rite are engaged in or not (and many times they are not enacted), this is, no doubt, the time of year sending Wiccans in search of all forms of abundance and fertility which can begin to take root. In ancient times, many cultures saw their Kings or Queens, who would symbolically hold the power of the God or Goddess, join in a symbolic union (generally, the physical union was not open for witnesses). This symbolic union of marriage would ensure fertility in nature by joining the masculine and feminine energies of the Divine through human vessels. This alliance would later evolve into more of a political tactic as royalty would marry to secure land ownership or support in later battles. The marriage of the God and Goddess on Beltane is a sacred union and one that will regenerate the future harvest, allowing continued survival on earth.

Witches practice long-held traditions on this day. Traditions include handfastings (Wiccan marriages) and dancing around the Maypole (a tradition symbolizing fertility and the joining together of opposite forces). Beltane is the day to celebrate fertility and abundance in all its forms, and all Magickal workings involving abundance, prosperity, and happiness are traditional practices on this day. The day involves rituals, feasting and traditional spring colors for decorative purposes. As this holiday lies opposite Samhain on the Witches' Wheel of the Year, it is not only the time of heightened growth and development, but it is the time where the veil between the realms is thinnest. Traditionally, it is a Magickal time and lends well to the practice of divination.

SUMMER SOLSTICE

ALTERNATIVE IDENTIFICATIONS
Litha, Midsummer

NORTHERN HEMISPHERE
June 20, 21, 22, or 23

SOUTHERN HEMISPHERE
December 20, 21, 22, or 23

SABBAT TYPE
Lesser

Religious Meaning: A solstice refers to the apparent distance between the earth and sun, marks the longest day in the Northern Hemisphere, and the shortest day in the Southern Hemisphere. This day marks the zenith of the light's growth during the year; daylight has increased steadily since Winter Solstice, representing the growing energy of the God of nature. His growing power has developed and matured, sought union with the Maiden Goddess and now is at the height of masculine energy and power. At this time, the God as Holly King and Oak King re-emerge to battle for control again. This time, the Holly King wins the battle and the world witnesses the decrease in daylight, symbolized by the defeat of the Oak King. In ancient times, as light decreased, the diminishment of light was symbolically evident in the act of choosing a new leader or in rites of celebration where participants re-enacted the battles between the Oak and Holly King. Such reenactments were more pageant than serious battles however. During this season, all of nature has bloomed, fertility and abundance surround humankind, and hopes and spirits are soaring with the energy of prolonged daylight and growth. The season reminds Witches that the climax in the light season has come.

Witches realize as the cycle continues, just as the strong youthful Oak King is defeated by the older, wiser, Holly King, so too will humankind begin the slow process of settling down and preparing for the dark season to return. At this time, there is still time to reap the abundance of a fertile harvest before the arrival of winter. The symbolic defeat of the Oak King carries the message that all of life changes and one will, at some point, lose their youth to old age, or one may at some point witness abundance giving way to scarcity, but these conditions are transient and part of the great cycle of life.

In the meantime, summer is in full bloom and Wiccans celebrate appropriately with decorations reminiscent of the beautiful bounty offered up by the land. Some Wiccans will choose to celebrate outdoors, or at least will decorate their sacred space with the flowers of summer, seashells, or other reminders of things they enjoy about the season. Rituals performed honor the height of the Sun God's glory and strength, while acknowledging after this date the God will slowly wane in strength and return at Yule.

Witches praise the Goddess in this season in Her guise as the Mother Goddess who, impregnated on Beltane by the God, symbolically brings life to all of nature through her fertility and abundance. Other rituals include attracting growth and abundance in the life of the practitioner, harnessing the heightened solar energy for works of healing, rituals to spark inspiration and hope, as well as honoring the maternal and paternal forces in nature. This is a time to reflect on the growing aspects of one's life with hopefulness and gratitude. Decorative colors are light and may include yellows and other bright colors in honor of the sun.

Traditionally, this day has also been associated with strong Magickal workings and even a little trickster energy. Shakespeare's play, *A Midsummer Night's Dream,* exemplifies the themes of Summer Solstice, in which the playwright combines the themes of love, lust, and merriment with an element of faery Magick and trickster energy. It is no wonder Shakespeare chose this season for the setting and title of his play, as this is a time when the light and joyful energy often associated with faeries and other elementals are more accessible due to the excitement and hope experienced by humans in the long daylight hours.

LAMMAS

ALTERNATIVE IDENTIFICATIONS
Bread Harvest, Lughnasadh

NORTHERN HEMISPHERE
August 1 & 2

SOUTHERN HEMISPHERE
February 1 & 2

SABBAT TYPE
Greater

Religious Meaning: After the Summer Solstice, one will find another Cross Quarter day before the final equinox of the year: This is Lammas, a marker of early autumn. Traditionally, this holiday also harkens the beginning of early harvest, usually of fruit. The waning summer brings Lammas and the holiday helps practitioners prepare for the coming of Autumn. The Goddess and God transitioning from the growth season into the harvest season is a spiritual parallel. There is a transition in nature as well as all of life begins to slow its pace and to prepare for winter.

Rituals held at this time of year may call for the reflection on what the practitioner has spiritually "grown" this season and what may have been unintentionally brought to harvest; this reflection later results in the cleansing and purification in preparation for the harvest season. This is also a time to begin giving thanks for the blessings of summer and the harvest.

Witches decorate sacred space with markers of the season, and harvested plants or flowers, or herbs in preparation for drying. This is also a nice time to transition from the bright colors of summer to more muted tones, although decoration depends also on personal preference. The Goddess and God, in the aspect of Mother and Father of nature, are developing into the Crone and Sage Divine aspects, and practitioners, aligned with the shifts in nature, are aware of the change in the energies. Traditionally, this is an ideal time to take inventory of supplies, to harvest for the coming winter, and to prepare if the season fell short in providing a fruitful harvest. Magickally, one can still take inventory of what they have or have not managed to cultivate in their personal life and the practitioner can use the personal/spiritual assessment to make adjustments so spiritual progress/physical growth can be achieved.

FALL EQUINOX

ALTERNATIVE IDENTIFICATIONS
Autumnal Equinox, Mabon

NORTHERN HEMISPHERE
September 20, 21, 22, or 23

SOUTHERN HEMISPHERE
March 20, 21, 22, or 23

SABBAT TYPE
Lesser

Religious Meaning: As the daylight waned from Summer Solstice, once again all is in balance between light and dark on Autumnal Equinox. As promised in the defeat of the Oak King at Summer Solstice, the dark will once again "conquer" the light. This equinox marks the point of balance with day and nighttime being equal. Symbolically, the powers of the growing and waning forces of nature are in a temporary state of equality before all of nature decays into darkness for the winter. Witches thank the God and Goddess for the harvest, literally and symbolically. This holiday is the Wiccan equivalent of Thanksgiving. It reminds Wiccans of their many blessings and the fortunate abundance found in all of nature. This same abundance is apparent again in the regeneration of nature as the cycle continues. The Witches' Wheel of the Year signifies the seasons, the cycles of life, and Wiccans honor both. As the year has moved from Samhain to Fall Equinox, the year is soon ending and the yearly cycle will begin again with the arrival of Samhain.

The Fall Equinox reminds Wiccans that while energy waxes and wanes throughout the year, it is also important to strive toward balance at all times. This is the height of the harvest time, when people harvest and store vegetables and grains for the long season ahead. Fall colors make great decorations for these rites, yellows, oranges, browns and greens bring the energies of fall to the Wiccan altar. Witches like to use colored leaves, pinecones, dried herbs, and other symbolic representations found right in the natural world such as grape vine wreaths and the flowers of summer in their dried forms, preserved and representing the endurance through the season ahead. Wiccans may choose season appropriate foods for their post ritual feasts.

Practitioners, blessed with abundance, share the abundance with the community through works of charity, donations, and other means of giving back to society, although such actions are not solely for this time of year. Wiccans celebrate abundance, and then prepare for the season of reflection and challenges to come. Although the days begin to decrease in length after Summer Solstice, they have maintained longevity over nighttime up until the arrival of Fall Equinox, when both are temporarily equal, and then the darkness of night will once again resume its reign; the nocturnal energies increase until Yule when the cycle will change once more.

Tools of The Craft: an offering bowl, gypsy pot, seashell, charm bag, and a piece of lava.

ADDITIONAL RITES AND PRACTICES

While Wiccans celebrate eight specific holidays throughout the year, this in no way prevents them from celebrating other holidays with their friends and family. While a Wiccan is not Christian, it does not mean they cannot enjoy holidays like Easter or Christmas so they can share time with their loved ones. While the Christian holidays or holidays from other religions have different symbolic meanings, it is perfectly acceptable for a Wiccan to enjoy the traditions of other religious-oriented holidays. Instead of viewing such holidays for their religious connotations, Wiccans participate in holiday celebrations to spend quality time with family members, to share in the act of giving, and to express their love for loved ones. The opposite is also true, non-Wiccans may find themselves as guests at a sabbat with Wiccan loved ones, without having to compromise their beliefs or values.

ESBATS

Depending upon the amount of space available to practitioners or the location, esbats occur indoors or out. Witches gather during esbats when it is possible to do so and solitary practitioners often practice esbats alone. In today's world, many of us have jobs that may interfere with the timing of esbats, so sometimes coven practitioners may have to perform esbats solo. Esbats are a time when practitioners gather during a full moon and pay reference to patron deities or to various aspects of the Divine. They are not worshipping the moon however. Instead, Witches worship what the moon represents. Wiccans draw down the moon's energies during esbat to aid in Magickal workings, and they give thanks for the blessings they receive. Witches also pay honor to the God and Goddess, although the Goddess receives more

The Goddess of the moon, and an air dragon.

emphasis during esbats since the moon is a symbolic representation of the Feminine Divine just as the sun is a symbolic representation of the Masculine Divine. During esbats, practitioners attune themselves to the cycles of the earth and moon, remember who they are, and to remember their devotion to the Divine and their purpose here on earth. Esbat rites involve meditations, grounding, visualizations, spell workings, and prayers, too.

Esbats often involve the use of the same tools used for celebrating the sabbats. The practices occurring during esbats sometimes differ however; the practitioner may or may not open a Magick circle, depending upon preference. Some practitioners make esbat practices as elaborate as sabbat rituals. Often the Goddess is invoked (called upon for their assistance and presence in the rite), one's ritual intent is expressed; practitioners "draw down moon energies," Magickal workings are performed, and sometimes practitioners have cakes, ale, or other foods and beverages. As always, the practitioner thanks the deities for their presence and assistance in the rite, and if a practitioner constructs a Magick circle, he or she releases it.

WICCANINGS

Wiccanings are rites of passage. The Wiccaning ritual is the rite a practitioner uses when parents decide to request protection from the God and Goddess for a child. This rite is akin to a Christian baptism rite, but there are distinct differences. The child does not become a Wiccan via a Wiccaning. The practitioner requests protective energies and Divine intervention for the child through the child's life journey. After a Wiccaning, the child is not obligated to become Wiccan later on in life. In some cases, the parents of the child may choose adult guardians, sometimes Pagan and sometimes not, to serve as guides for the child in his or her lifetime.

HANDFASTINGS

Handfastings are equivalent to marriage rites; this is a joining of two consenting adults in marriage. In some instances, the vows between the couple last for a year and a day period. After the year and a day, the couple can renew their commitment to one another or they can part ways. In other cases, a Pagan officiant, a legally registered Priest or Priestess performs a handfasting (where it is legal to do so). In such instances, the marriage is permanent, and legally binding, unless the couple chooses to divorce.

CROSSINGS/BANISHINGS

Sometimes Wiccans help those who are deceased and earth bound cross over to the Summerlands. Spirits, through various rites, are encouraged to cross over and continue on their spiritual journey. The process does not involve provocation. The goal is to guide the spirit in the right direction with a gentle and compassionate approach. Some Wiccans believe that a person cannot force spirits to cross over if they do not desire to leave.

Banishings involve the removal of negative spiritual energies or entities. The goal of a banishing is to clear an area of chaotic, negative forces and to reunify the energies so they are positive. Banishings allow for the reunification of chaotic energies and the practitioner(s) does not banish positive spirits during the process.

ASTRAL PROJECTION

Wiccans often work with astral projection. This is a practice of entering into a state of altered awareness, either achieved through naturally entering a lucid dream state or a trancelike state achieved through prolong meditation, so one can "separate" from the physical body and travel in the astral realms; this is also identified as an out of body experience. The astral realm, sometimes called the astral sphere, world, or plane, is a plane that exists at a higher frequency or vibration. The superimposition of the Astral sphere over the physical plane allows for interaction between the two planes.

DREAM INTERPRETATION

Some Wiccans maintain dream journals. Dreams are documented in a journal or tape/digital recordings and later analyzed so any symbolic messaged conveyed via the subconscious (or sometimes through spirit communications) can be interpreted and applied to one's life. In some cases, Wiccans also believe spirits can communicate with the practitioner through dreams, and that a dreamer can sometimes receive Divine messages.

SPELLS

Before a Wiccan can begin the art of spell casting, a strong foundation in Witchcraft basics is required; this will help prevent backfiring, or unexpected repercussions when working with Magick. No one should ever dabble in Magick. When a practitioner is in doubt about any measure, the practitioner should refrain from doing anything until they are certain about what needs to be done or they have contacted a trustworthy, experienced practitioner for advice.

Witches cast spells for a variety of reasons, but if they are adhering to the Wiccan Rede, such reasons are always positive. Witches believe the words used in spell casting must be specific, precise, and unambiguous to avoid any unwanted outcomes. One's intent must be strong and the practitioner must not doubt the power of his or her Magick. Doubting the Magick weakens the spells power thereby influencing the spell's outcome. Spell workings can include spells for protection, prosperity, abundance, fertility, health, bringing positive energies into one's life, and for many other positive purposes. As mentioned earlier, many Wiccans frown upon the utilization of love

Tools of the Craft: Statues of Isis, Anubis, and Bast; incense, feathers, offering bowl, candles, crystals, herbs, and totems. *Courtesy of Sathish Vijayan.*

spells since using such spells infringes upon the free will of another. Spells that are general, seeking love in one's life, and not aimed at a specific person are acceptable.

Sometimes Wiccans use poppets (small handmade dolls) in spell work; a Wiccan does not use poppets to hurt others. A Witch uses poppets for spells involving healing. A spell's power is akin to the power of prayer. The will and intent of the practitioner powers the spell. If the practitioner's intent is positive, then the Magickal workings are equally positive. Witches also believe the more congruent spell components are with the goal of the work, the more powerful the spell is; the practitioner's intent, the components of the spell, the spell's timing, the Magickal correspondences used, and the practitioner's continued actions after the spell working all unify to determine a spell's success.

DIVINATION

Wiccans often use different forms of divination for the purposes of predicting future events. Predictions provide a chance to see upcoming obstacles and challenges: This gives the practitioner a chance to prepare for what lies ahead, to make decisions based

Tools used for divination: a handmade scrying mirror, and a crystal ball.

upon potential outcomes, and to enhance the fluidity of life's many events. Divination include the use of scrying (gazing) into a crystal ball, a bowl of water, candle flame, or mirror; the use of Tarot cards, astrology, bibliomancy (diving with random book passages), numerology, runes, the I Ching, Palmistry (palm reading), and tea leaves, among others. Wiccans do not believe the use of divinatory tools is evil and the use of divinatory methods does not involve negative entities, spirits, or forces.

HEALING WORK

Many Wiccans utilize natural or alternative healing methods to perform healing work. Some Wiccans specialize in herbology and the use of natural herbs for healing, while other Wiccans enjoy the use of Reiki (hands on healing and the use of universal energies for healing). In other cases, when Wiccans draw down the moon (a ritual where the Goddess is invoked), the Goddess's energies can be utilized for the purposes of healing or positive works. Other forms of healing Wiccans may use include the use of Reflexology, chromotherapy or color therapy, homeopathy, acupressure, acupuncture, massage, psychic healing, and Energy Medicine, among others.

SPIRIT COMMUNICATION

Many Wiccans engage in spirit communication. As mentioned earlier, bear in mind not all Wiccans use Ouija boards or engage in séances in order to communicate with spirits, and some Wiccans firmly assert the dangers in using the latter methods of spirit communication. The question to whether or not automatic writing is a safe practice sometimes arises. During an automatic writing session, a spirit takes over the bodily control or consciousness of the individual and causes the individual to write down messages from the spirit. Some people believe that the process opens the practitioner up to potential possession by a spirit, thereby making the process dangerous.

Wiccans work on improving their innate psychic abilities including clairvoyance (clear seeing), clairaudience (clear hearing), and clairsentience (clear sensing). Sometimes Wiccans rely on clairolfactory (clear smelling) and clairgustant (clear tasting) abilities too. A practitioner improves and enhances all of the latter mentioned psychic abilities via regular meditation and psychic exercises. Witches sometimes use psychometry to read an object, to discern something about a spirit connected to the object. Psychometry helps

Handmade pendulum board used for spirit communication and divination.

the practitioner "read" the object to discern the object's history or to connect with a person or an object's owner. Psychometry involves the placement of one's hands on an object to see what psychic impressions one draws from holding the object. Meanwhile, some Witches will use pendulums or dowsing rods to detect the presence of spirits, and pendulums in particular can prove a good method for communicating with spirits.

In every instance, when working with spirits, Wiccans use proper protections. Often, a Witch uses white light visualization to protect him or herself from negative energies or the Witch requests protection from the Divine. Sometimes Witches use amulets and protection spells for protection from psychic or physical attacks as well.

CREATIVITY

By tapping into one's creative side, one can develop a deeper connection with the Divine. Thus, many Wiccans partake of creative endeavors including drawing, painting, writing, sculpting, crafts, and other artistic endeavors. Even if a person doesn't feel artistically inclined, he or she can still be creatively inspired on the job, at school, or when dealing with mundane tasks of any kind.

WICCAN TENETS AND PRINCIPLES

Many Wiccan tenets stem from a variety of literary works or from documents created by various Pagan organizations. Wiccan tenets are in a variety of books and many tenets are available online. For more information, the reader can examine the suggested reading list and Internet resources provided at the end of this book. Since other books have already covered Wiccan tenets, a terse summary of the tenets and guiding principles follows here so the reader can become familiar with them. A brief review of the different documents, literature, and of the basic understandings of Wicca will reveal much about the kinds of beliefs Wiccans hold.

THE THIRTEEN GOALS OF A WITCH

The American Witch and author Scott Cunningham, in his book *Wicca: A Guide for the Solitary Practitioner*, first presented the "Thirteen Goals of a Witch." The tenets suggest Witches strive for self-knowledge and Craft-knowledge. It also recommends that

Witches work toward learning the wise application of the knowledge they acquire. The tenets put forward that Witches need to care for the body and mind, to be observant of actions and thoughts, to attune to earth's cycles, to rejoice in life's blessings, and to honor the Divine.[2] These tenets give all Wiccans guidelines on how to live a spiritually fulfilling life as well as practical instructions for living a satisfying life on the physical plane.

THE PRINCIPLES OF BELIEF

The Council of American Witches, a now defunct group, devised the "Principles of Belief" which consist of thirteen guidelines Wiccans follow; the set of guidelines encourage Wiccans to attune to earthly cycles, to behave in an environmentally friendly manner, and to strive for balance in all things.[3] In addition, it explains Witches believe in and acknowledge spiritual worlds, the innate psychic abilities belonging to all people; Witches maintain no belief in the devil, Wiccans are not anti-Christian, and bearing certain titles or degrees does not make a person a Witch, but living the lifestyle of a Witch does.[4] The latter beliefs are popular among Wiccans today, and the guidelines set forth in the "Principles of Belief," are reiterated and reinforced by other Wiccan tenets.

THE LAW OF POWER

"The Law of Power" by Scott Cunningham is in his book: *Living Wicca: A Further Guide for the Solitary Practitioner.* These tenets suggest Wiccans should not use Magick in hurtful ways; practitioners use Magickal abilities when deemed necessary and appropriate; the acceptance of monies for the use of one's powers is inappropriate, and Magickal abilities are a sacred gift from the Divine.[5] In essence, the tenets explain the proper use of Magickal abilities and the need to view the Magickal Arts as sacred.

MAGICAL PRINCIPLES

The Magical Principles are in *Cunningham's Encyclopedia of Magical Herbs*. These principles are similar to the assertions set forth in the other tenets the author has established. The guidelines explain how Witches view Magickal practices as natural; the use of Magick requires dedicated effort, and the practitioner's effort defines the Magickal outcome. The tenets also suggest Magick can be used for the purposes of protection, but such practices are not to be used to cause harm to others or for vengeful purposes; best of all, the tenets propose all Magickal practices should be based in acts of love.[6] As it is with all Wiccan tenets, there is an emphasis on love, honor, dignity, respect, and reverence.

THE EARTH RELIGION ANTI-ABUSE RESOLUTION

The Church of All Worlds drafted "The Earth Religion Anti-Abuse Resolution" in the late 1980s. The document explains followers of the Wiccan faith, along with other Pagan and Earth-oriented religions, do not condone abuse of any kind.[7] The document also asserts Pagans revere the earth and engage in healing, compassionate acts, and that Wiccans do not pay reverence to Satan.[8] Again, by reviewing the latter tenets it becomes clear the Wiccan faith has nothing to do with negative practices.

THE THREE-FOLD LAW OF RETURN

The Three-fold Law of Return, sometimes called the Three-Fold Law, The Law of Three, or the Rule of Three, is the basic understanding that whatever a person does comes back to the individual times three. Thus, if someone acts in harmful ways, either intentionally or unintentionally, the negative energies sent forth into the universe will return onto the individual multiplied. The three-fold law serves as a moral compass and allows the practitioner to consider the consequences of their actions before taking any action at all.

THE WITCHES' REDE OF CHIVALRY

"The Witches' Rede of Chivalry" is a code of conduct offered in the *Magical Rites from the Crystal Well* by Ed Fitch. The code encourages Witches to behave in honorable ways, to respect the ancient deities, to recognize the power of the mind, to be true to one's self, to refrain from gossip, to be truthful, and to refrain from allowing irrational emotions to control what one does.[9] Witches are further encouraged to consider the consequences of every action, to respect other Witches and covens, to respect individual differences, to act with dignity, to be gracious, to have a sense of humor, and to honor the self, others, and the Divine.[10] The tenets set forth in the Rede of Chivalry reiterate the practical guidance set forth in other Pagan/Wiccan codes of conduct.

THE CHARGES OF THE GODDESS AND GOD

There are a few different versions of the Charge of the Goddess and the Charge of the God, but the text conveys the instructive guidance for those paying reverence to the Feminine or Masculine Divine; one of the most popular versions of "The Charge" is by Doreen Valiente. A similar variant of Valiente's Charge appears in

Statue of the Goddess Diana. *Courtesy of Justyn Staley.*

Janet and Stewart Farrar's work (*A Witches Bible*). No matter who authored "The Charge," it is usually a poem, and the cumulative passages explain the need for monthly reverence of the Goddess during esbats. In addition, for those honoring the Goddess, the rewards are enlightenment and a deep understanding of the mysteries. The Charge also explains Wiccans should strive for excellence, and to exhibit honorable and compassionate behaviors. Finally, the closing of "The Charge of the Goddess" conveys the eminence of the Feminine Divine.

THE WITCHES' CREED

"The Witches'Creed" is a poem by the Witch and author Doreen Valiente. It appears in her book *Witchcraft for Tomorrow* and it is sometimes confused with the Witches' Rede. The Witches' Creed is a poem consisting of sixteen quatrains and a final rhyming couplet. It explains how present-day Witches are no longer hiding who they are. It also explains how Witches acknowledge and work with the elements as well as how Witches celebrate the seasons, the earth cycles, and life.[11] The poem additionally covers information about sabbats, esbats, innate Magickal abilities, how Magickal understandings have been passed down through the generations, circle casting, the need to respect what is sacred, and how and why Wiccans honor the Feminine and Masculine Divine. The final rhyming couplet of the poem is the best remembered because it tells of our single mandate to harm no one.[12] Many Wiccans focus on the final stanza when expressing their beliefs; the "harm none" stanza is the most important stanza in the entire poem, but its importance does not negate the equal importance of the rest of what the poem expresses.

THE WICCAN REDE

Credited to Doreen Valiente, Gerald Gardner, or Lady Gwen Thompson, The Wiccan Rede's origins are highly debated. Doreen Valiente's version, a poem, has eight words that are the most significant:

Eight words the Wiccan Rede fulfill — / an' it harm none do what ye will.[13]

The Rede explains how Witches work with one another in a state of "perfect trust," how Witches give and take fairly, why the

Magick circle is used, why spells are written in rhyming format, when and why certain Magickal practices are performed, and describes Wiccan celebrations throughout the year. The poem even references the widely adhered to threefold law of return.[14] Once again, the philosophies Wiccans embrace are clearly absent of evil or negative connotations.

THE HARM NONE RULE DEBATE

Some practitioners will argue the "harm none" rule is an impossible rule to follow since there are situations in everyday life where it is impossible to avoid harming someone, even when the practitioner is seemingly doing the right thing in a given situation. When it comes to the Magickal Arts, the "harm none," rule can indeed be adhered to, provided the practitioner consider all the consequences of his or her actions before using Magick. The key here is considering *all* consequences; if the practitioner fails to foresee a potential outcome of their actions, then the result of their actions can still potentially lead to harm. It is simple enough to decide not to cast curses, hexes, or to use Magick irresponsibly. Things can become more complex however, if a practitioner is learning about Magickal practices via experimentation, and the practitioner harms someone or one's self unintentionally. The problem is, every practitioner is an imperfect human being capable of making mistakes that can result in harm.

The "harm none" rule is a philosophy, one that always needs to be considered while working Magick; the rule exists so practitioners can potentially avoid deliberately or unintentionally using Magick in baneful ways, but due to human imperfections and the imperfections existent in reality, on occasion the rule is broken. This is not to say there are not karmic repercussions the practitioner faces, and the Three-fold Law of Return ensures the practitioner will receive whatever he or she puts forth, whether the practitioner's initial actions were willful or not. Additionally, while it is true some mundane situations in life may put a practitioner in a position where they end up harming someone unintentionally, it is important for the practitioner to make every effort to avoid harming someone. In mundane situations where a practitioner has to choose between "the lesser of two evils," in order to achieve the most appropriate outcome, the practitioner has still made every effort to "harm none," in the process.

In reality, humans are fallible, they live in an imperfect world in a real-world setting; the best the practitioner can do is to make every effort to adhere to the "harm none" rule whenever it is possible to do so. This does not make the "harm none" rule one the practitioner can either take or leave at one's whim; rather, the rule is something each practitioner strives to maintain in an effort to make the most of every life situation and every Magickal endeavor. The "harm none" rule is a guide; a philosophy every practitioner aspires to when using Magick or when interacting with all things in the mundane world. The word *rede* means, "council, advice, consideration, a guiding principle, or a standard one or more people choose to follow," one requiring thoughtful reflection, contemplation, and one tempered by logic.[15] Here is the bottom line: The *rede* is a guide, and it is not something Divinely mandated; it is however, something one must always consider in the light of any given situation or Magickal practice.

Additional Basic Guidelines and Beliefs

Reincarnation and Karma

Many Wiccans believe in reincarnation; they believe one lifetime is not enough to learn all there is about the universe. The belief in reincarnation also includes the understanding that one chooses who he or she will be in this lifetime and the lessons to learn. Coupled with the belief in reincarnation, is the concept of the three-fold law and karma. Wiccans believe every action influences a person's karma, and if they do not experience the repercussions of negative actions in this present lifetime, they will experience the repercussions in future life times. Thus, bad actions will eventually revisit the practitioner. Consequences of inappropriate action are lessons to learn from in this lifetime or in future lifetimes. Wiccans believe unlearned lessons become repetitious; until the individual learns from lessons, he or she will have experiences with similar themes. Unlearned lessons can carry on into future lifetimes as well. Once mastered however, the individual moves on to the next lesson.

The Divine in All

The belief governing a Wiccan's understandings is that the Divine polarity of the Goddess and God reside in all living things. Wiccans strive to respect the Divine in every being and they understand all beings have something to teach. Wiccans see the earth and all of nature as a manifestation of the Divine on the physical plane. Thus, they honor and respect all of nature and the world.

Sun and Moon wall plaque from Mexico: another representation of the God and Goddess.

SPIRITUAL PATHS AND INDIVIDUALITY

Wiccans believe everyone has the right to choose the spiritual path right for them. There is no rigid hierarchy or dogma governing Witches and there are countless traditions in the faith. Each Wiccan chooses his or her own spiritual path, chooses the deities he or she honors, and each individual is responsible for his or her own actions.

VISUALIZATION AND ITS POWER

Wiccans firmly believe in the power derived from visualization. While many Witches invest in tools and some of the trappings of Witchcraft are nice to have, the tools are merely "extras." True Magick comes from the practitioner, his or her intent, the ability to visualize, and the focus on energies in order to cause change in the physical plane. Daily meditation helps to strengthen the practitioner's visualization skills too. In truth, no physical tools are necessary when it comes to Magickal practices, but many Witches choose to either make or buy their tools.

THE ADVANTAGES OF BEING WICCAN

There are many advantages a practitioner derives from being Wiccan. If a practitioner remains dedicated to The Craft, to studying, and to applying Wiccan principles to one's everyday existence, the individual can align him or herself with Magickal energies. In doing so, dramatic, and positive changes can and do occur.

The first advantage a person derives from being Wiccan is a deep, established connection with the Divine. A Wiccan often feels Divinely guided, and this lends to a deep sense of spiritual fulfillment. Wiccans learn to recognize animal messages, Divine messages in mundane experiences, to interpret synchronistic events, and to use innate abilities in order to understand existence on a mundane level with greater clarity. Thus, the Wiccan world view allows practitioners to add a more intense layer of meaning to day-to-day existence. The connection to the subconscious or higher self, the connection to spirit guides, and the understanding of dreams enhances a Witch's life. Wiccans recognize the Divine existing in all things. What's more, Wiccans, realizing their connection to all other living things, develop deeper empathic bonds with people and animals. A practitioner also understands that actions affect all things connected to a practitioner in a "ripple-like" effect.

The Wiccan world view allows practitioners to appreciate the world, animals, and all blessings, both big and small. Through ritual workings, Wiccans become closer to the Divine. Through spell casting, they can see the direct results of their actions. This gives a sense of far greater control over life events, and it allows Wiccans to take personal responsibility for who they are, who they become, their life direction, and what they do. Wiccans develop a level of self-awareness allowing them to make life improvements. Witches are encouraged to "know thyself," to examine one's actions and motives, and to use such assessments to make appropriate life changes and choices. What's more, the adherence to the Rule of Three or the Threefold Law of Return allows Wiccans to establish a rigid moral compass; thus, practitioners can lead ethical and fulfilling lifestyles that are oriented on positive actions and workings. With a greater sense of life control, Wiccans often gain greater self-esteem, self-confidence, and as the Magickal skills of practitioners improve and evolve, their spiritual path parallels such an evolution. What's more, since Wiccans acknowledge innate psychic abilities, they harness tools that intensify their interaction with and understanding of the mundane plane. Wiccans also get the chance to experience energies many people either refuse to acknowledge or do not know how to utilize.

Wiccans benefit from practicing meditation in myriad ways. The use of meditation allows a practitioner to improve thinking processes, to learn how to turn within for inner guidance, and to relax both the mind and body. Additional benefits derived from meditation include, but are not limited to an improved overall sense of well being, an improved sense of inner harmony and balance, an improved ability for focus and concentration, and the ability to heal the self is improved, as is the ability to address day-to-day issues with greater clarity and confidence.

ARE THERE DISADVANTAGES TO BEING WICCAN?

Wicca is a positive religion, but it is wrong to assume there are no disadvantages associated with being Wiccan. Myriad issues can arise, starting from the moment when an individual begins to decide if Wicca is the appropriate path. Making the decision to be Wiccan is a weighty choice, especially if a person chooses to let the world know about his or her religious predilection. The practitioner may face religious persecution and the identity of people who illustrate upset with one's religious choices may prove surprising. Family, friends, associates, or even strangers may criticize a Wiccan. There are many reasons why a Wiccan may encounter disapproval from others. For example, a person might not know what Wicca is; a person may not be accepting of the faith; a person may view one's beliefs in direct opposition of his or her faith, or the individual who is criticizing a Wiccan might believe the criticism offered is for the individual's own good or spiritual well-being.

Sometimes Wiccans fear losing friends, family, their job, their homes, or custody of their children because they have chosen a religion often not openly accepted by everyone. Occasionally, being open about being Wiccan can make the practitioner well-known in the community, and despite the fact it is illegal to discriminate against a person for their religion, one may find it more difficult to make friends with others, to rent an apartment, to get or keep a job, or to advance in an existing job position. Some people are candid when offering opposition to Wiccan beliefs. A Witch might even experience incidents where a person accosts and ridicules him or her in a public setting. In some cases, people who meet a practitioner will not think twice about expressing personal opinions regarding Wiccan beliefs. A person might confront a Wiccan on the Internet, via email, chat rooms, and public forums. In contrast, a person sometimes implies their opposition to Wiccan beliefs via off-hand remarks, comments, and not-so-subtle innuendos.

In social circles, people sometimes change their views of an individual who is Wiccan. If a Witch has children, people may question the practitioner's parenting abilities. Skewed views about Witchcraft can also affect a practitioner's children. Some non-Wiccan parents, in an effort to protect their own children from perceived undesirable influences, may forbid them interacting with someone with different religious beliefs. If it is a child or teen with Wiccan beliefs, again the child could be isolated because he or she has engaged in religious practices not considered acceptable by some followers of more mainstream religions, or the child might be marked as a "bad influence."

Sometimes solitary practitioners have a hard time finding a support system in the community. As a solitary, a Witch might lack the interaction one can get when working within a coven. Meanwhile, if a solitary practitioner is seeking a coven to work with, it can take a while for the practitioner to find one that welcomes him or her and makes the individual comfortable. If a practitioner has trouble establishing a support system, he or she may have unanswered questions about Wiccan practices or the practitioner may have doubts about some aspects of The Craft that go unaddressed. The solitary practitioner also often lacks the "strength in numbers" that comes with being a coven member; a Witch can benefit from having like-minded individuals to turn to when issues regarding religious intolerance arise.

In terms of the Wiccan community, both novices and adepts occasionally come across ongoing Witch Wars: battles between solitary Witches or conflicts between covens within the same communities. These wars involve arguments over traditions, practices, beliefs, or they involve the egocentric positions of practitioners. Unfortunately, when Witch Wars do occur, the resulting actions do not parallel Wiccan beliefs since acts of Magickal vengeance or public displays of opposition often result: This is in direct opposition to the "harm none," rule. What's more, the antagonistic atmosphere created in Witch Wars is not conducive to Magickal practices. A practitioner degrades and taints his or her Magick; it does not help the practitioner spiritually evolve, and the negative energies that result can attract more energies that are negative.

If practiced with haste, with poor judgment, or with lack of knowledge or experience, Magickal practices can backfire in harmful ways. Magick is not something to play or experiment with, and the same goes for spirit communication, the invocation of deities or elementals, and other parts of the Wiccan practices that, to a novice, may seem exciting, tantalizing, entertaining, or harmless fun. Magick, when performed badly or without acknowledgement of potential repercussions can result in the attraction of negative energies. In addition, lack of knowledge and experience may make the difference between a positive healing ritual and a ritual resulting in the attraction of potentially negative spirits.

A careless practitioner can misinterpret Wiccan practices. Misinterpretations of Magickal practices can result in erroneous application. If a practitioner uses Magick in haste, for the wrong reasons, for recklessly calling on spiritual beings and elements, or the practitioner toys with herbs or Magick tools without knowledge about their proper usage, a ritual or spell can backfire. Magick can prove harmful if the practitioner does not know what they are doing. An imagined example would be someone who is learning Wicca with no outside guidance. With only positive intentions, the novice starts reading about The Craft and decides to practice a little spell; the practitioner cannot find any *good* spells in a book so they decide to make one up from scratch. To start, the practitioner begins walking in a counter clockwise circle without recognizing that walking widdershins attracts banishing energies. The practitioner hopes to resolve a conflict at their job, so he or she focuses on work to end the conflict. The Witch has some knowledge of Magickal tools, and begins to chant words in another language without knowledge of what the words mean. The novice does not realize it, but he or she has not cast any type of circle for protection, has walked in a direction associated with "undoing," perhaps chants things not intended or absent of specificity, and has focused on banishing a conflict at work. It would not be any surprise if the practitioner went into work and was laid off or fired. The spell did solve the conflict at work, but not the way the person really desired. Meanwhile, the novice would wonder how things could have backfired.

A Witch must base the decision to become Wiccan on the understanding that there is a significant amount of work involved in living a Wiccan lifestyle. Being Wiccan involves practice, tremendous study, discipline, and commitment. The individual must desire to evolve physically and spiritually. The practitioner must be equally willing to challenge existing knowledge at every turn. A willingness to learn about Wiccan fundamentals, Magickal theories, and a willingness to learn about alternative religions is also necessary. When studying other systems of belief, one challenges and strengthens his or her beliefs. Wiccans should in no way close themselves off to exploring the teachings of alternative religions.

Learning about symbolic interpretations is more difficult for some than others; this can prove problematic when involved in a religion that is easier to understand when the practitioner has a thorough grasp of archetypes, symbols, omens, synchronicities, and Divine messages. While some people develop an intricate understanding of symbols, others may have greater difficulty fully understanding the various connotations associated with religious symbolism, dreams, and the like. What's more, a willingness to learn about various symbols is not quite enough: The practitioner not only needs to know what certain symbols mean, but also how they can be applied in different circumstances where such symbols may prove instructive or meaningful.

Television and media continue to perpetuate myths about Witchcraft; this may be unintentional as the basis for media's success is high ratings. Television and movie ratings increase when presentations are shocking or dramatic. Being Wiccan forces the practitioner to regularly deal with the misunderstandings people develop after viewing media that has incorrectly presented Wicca and its traditions.

A practitioner has to handle every situation that arises with patience; in fact, when it comes to patience, a Wiccan requires a tremendous amount. A practitioner needs to be patient while attempting to achieve and maintain balance in every day existence. Patience is required during study, while using Magick, and a Wiccan has to develop patience for other people, too. It may seem unfair, but even when reacting to religious intolerance, a Wiccan has to "take the high road," and he or she must consider his or her reactions carefully. After all, actions define an individual, and if reacting to oppression with hostility, one falls into the trap of proving the opponent's arguments or illustrating that perhaps false accusations and intolerant remarks are true. Always considering the consequences of one's actions might seem easy, but when unfair circumstances fuel emotions, being conscious of all consequences becomes a far more difficult endeavor.

As will be explored in the last chapter of this book, sometimes a person's view of reality and mental stability are questioned when he or she chooses the Wiccan faith. Some of the traditions and beliefs Wiccans have seem unusual to individuals who do not fully understand Wiccan traditions. This can lead to issues where members of society unintentionally or deliberately question a practitioner's sense of reality. What's more, in extreme cases, religious hate crimes occur. One of the authors of this text was the victim of a religious hate crime when a person scrawled biblical passages and hateful words on the outside of her home. The passage read as follows:

> My Lord Heavenly Father, You are our creator, there is no one greater than you. Please My Lord, move Satan from this place, protect us from evil. The Lord is my Shepherd, I shall not want. He maketh me to lie down in green pastures. He leadeth me beside still waters, He restoreth my soul. He leadeth me on the path of righteousness for his namesake. Yea, though I walk through the valley of shadows of death, I will fear no evil, For thou art with me, thy rod and thy staff they comfort me. Thou preparest a table before me in the presence of my enemies. Thou anointst my head with oil, my cup runneth over. Surely goodness and mercy shall follow me all the days of my life and I will dwell in the house of the lord Forever, Amen. In the name of Jesus Christ, no evil witch or spook can attack my family. God is our protector, he is our creator, and no one is greater. Please move evil away. Amen.[16]

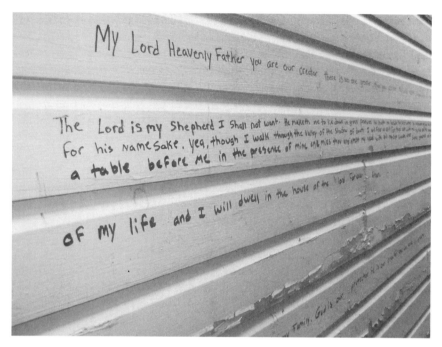

An incident of vandalism: hateful words scrawled on the outside wall of a Witch's home. *Courtesy of Phillip Gaudreau.*

It was not the Biblical verses that were hurtful, but the fact that the passages were written in an effort to intimidate the victim. Accompanying the biblical verse was the expressed desire for the victim to move away from the vicinity because she was a Witch and the passages equated her with Satan. Even worse, after reporting the crime to the police and following an investigation of the matter, the police have not found the perpetrators; the case remains unsolved.

Being a Witch can prove to be a problem with one's neighbors, with family members, or with friends. This is especially true if the Witch's practices are misunderstood. Finally, incidents similar to those mentioned earlier make it a far more difficult decision to come out of the proverbial broom closet and announce to the world one is a follower of the Wiccan faith.

CHAPTER 4

WHEN MAGICK IS SANE

*"Everybody likes to go their own way –
to choose their own time and manner of devotion."*

~Jane Austen

S ADLY, ON OCCASION, WITCHES HAVE people question their concept of reality. Wicca is different from many mainstream religions: This fact alone can prove problematic. More often than one might think, the dark side of the mental health profession has historically used its influence to marginalize those whose actions deviate greatly from accepted societal norms, behaviors, and beliefs. It is common for people to disregard or disparage Witches and their beliefs in the reality of Magick or other worldly realms. Sometimes, members of society view Witches as psychotic, disturbed, eccentric, bizarre, or a little "off" at best. Such assumptions are gravely erroneous, and it therefore becomes necessary to clarify the striking differences between what constitutes a mental illness and what constitutes religious predilection. Angela Kaufman, one of the coauthor's of this book, is a licensed social worker with over five years experience working with mentally ill clients. She has seen what happens when someone is truly

Close up view of a dragon censer and potion bottles.

psychotic or mentally unstable; such conditions in no way resemble the practices of a spiritually fulfilling, innocuous religion.

Religion and Culture Versus Diagnosable Illness

An important lesson is missing in the modern-day onslaught of commercials promoting the use of psychotropic drugs to cure all of one's mental ailments. Just as a cough does not equal pneumonia, a cultural or religious belief in Magick (or dragons, elves, faeries, psychic abilities, spirits, otherworldly realms) does not make a mental illness. A mental illness requires one to experience *maladaptive* symptoms, beliefs, or behaviors. The latter of which do not promote the health of the individual, and do not lend to the individual's progress toward developmentally appropriate goals. The symptoms one must present in order for one's beliefs and behaviors to prove a marker of mental illness must be severe, occurring to an extreme degree, and debilitating in some way. The symptoms must cause the individual distress and prohibit the person from engaging in developmentally appropriate

activities. In addition, in order for one's behaviors and beliefs to prove indicative of a mental illness, the symptoms must be dysfunctional leading to the impairment of personal and social functioning. Most importantly, the symptoms must pose a realistic danger to the individual's wellbeing or the wellbeing of others.

The symptoms of a mental illness would manifest in a person having a great deal of difficulty maintaining stability in work, relationships, and day-to-day tasks. The individual may also experience hallucinations, and cognitive distortions. Difficulty with social relationships can occur because the person's thoughts are so scattered and tend to be so illogical others have difficulty finding meaning in what the individual is trying to share or express. Others may have difficulty relating to the individual on a personal level as well. Over time, there would be an absence of friendships, the inability to remain employed, or potential health risks resulting from extreme isolation from most sources of social support. An individual who is cut off from close relationships, maintains unusual beliefs not attributable to culture or religion, and

An Oriental dragon, considered God-like, a Goddess statue, and a quartz crystal. Many Wiccans believe in the reality of otherworldly beings.

has highly dysfunctional behaviors, is the picture of a person suffering from a mental illness, not practicing a religion.

It is far more likely with the onset of a legitimate mental illness, like Schizophrenia for example, the individual will illustrate a marked period in his or her life considered "normal," followed by a period of time where a break with reality is evident and the onset of the disorder is clear. Someone with Schizophrenia or another type of mental illness would then show symptoms that reach beyond the existence of unusual perceptions or beliefs not based in reality or shared by others, and would include symptoms that cause a deficiency in the individual's ability to function in several areas of life without some medical/ psychological support or intervention. Ultimately, it is important to acknowledge that even the most unusual cultural/religious beliefs do not bear the same basic hallmarks of mental disorders.

Some individuals suffering from mental illness incorporate a religious belief or mild to moderate religious fixation along with their symptoms. In contrast, other individuals may find a religious faith helpful in recovering from otherwise distressing symptoms; for most individuals a spiritual belief system represents a source of stability and inspiration. Thus, one must always remember the importance of not confusing culture, traditions, and personal values with dysfunction just because they are rooted in a unique system of faith. With this understanding in mind, it becomes easier to see that any mental, behavioral, or physical symptoms that are debilitating, distressing, dysfunctional, and potentially dangerous do not resemble the criteria established in the Wiccan faith system. In fact, the Wiccan faith is a source of inspiration and spiritual strength for many.

Imagine a traditional Roman Catholic woman who exhibits intense devotion, and converses daily with God. She prays with the rosary regularly, seeks answers to life's questions from the Bible, attributes auspicious events to the intervention from saints, and she attributes unfortunate events to past behaviors she believes are sinful. Let's also suppose the woman has been motivated to care for her health, her family, and her neighbors because of her strong religious convictions which define decent and moral behavior; she takes care of her household, job, finances, and her religious beliefs serve as a source of comfort and inspiration. In this example, the woman's religious practices provide disciplined structure and her religiously defined principles enhance her life. While her practices appear as devotional overkill to her less religiously oriented friends and co-workers, her devotion and religious practices, while requiring time and effort, do not impair her ability to live a healthy, fulfilling life or cause any pathological degree of distress.

For the purposes of comparison, imagine a young man experiencing a hyper-religious state. For over a month, he has been experiencing extreme anxiety over the battle between heaven and hell, which he believes is fast approaching. At first, his friends support the basis of his fear, noting some social decline has indeed occurred in America over the years. Later, his friends become concerned with the young man's seemingly irrational preoccupation with apocalyptic ideations and they rarely visit. He begins locking himself in his apartment so no "devils" can get into his home. His fear becomes so irrational that soon he stops answering the phone because he believes God will only talk to him through the radio and any callers may really be the devil. As his mental aberrations increase, the young man stops eating in case his food is poisoned by the "devil's army," and believes prayer alone will keep him alive. He soon becomes so obsessed with religious rituals to keep the devil away that he seldom sleeps or showers. He loses his job due to absenteeism, his health and hygiene are poor, and he loses significant amounts of weight. In this extreme example, his symptoms are distortions of religious-based concepts and figures taken drastically out of context, and incorporated into a highly distorted, self-destructive view of reality that is not verifiable by any outside source as being consistent with facts. Even worse, he has endangered his own health.

The clear distinctions in the two imagined examples illustrate the difference between positive religious practices and how a mental illness can manifest in a way that incorporates religious ideas and beliefs, but is not the same as the tenets of the religion. In the example where a young man presents the hyper-religious symptoms, the inability to verify the factual basis for his beliefs is not even the issue: When it comes to consideration of a disturbed condition, the prominent factors are the compulsive, self-destructive, and damaging consequences of beliefs that prompts one to react in negative, antisocial, or in regressive ways.

Witches believe in Goddesses and Gods who interact with all forms of life. They also believe in animism (spirits found in human and nonhuman life), Magick (the ability to channel intent to change reality), and other concepts that often have not been accepted in mainstream culture. Wiccans believe in divination and in the ability to receive messages and guidance from animals, dreams, and signs. Still, a belief in any of these concepts does not share the properties of a mental illness.

Compare the first two examples offered to an imagined example of a female Wiccan who wakes early in the morning to start the day with a prayer and grounding meditation. The Witch performs prayer and meditation to cleanse her aura of negativity and to connect to the earth and the Divine. The individual goes through the morning routine and later arrives at work to find a new, frustrating project assigned. To manage the difficulty of the task, the individual silently prays to establish and sustain a connection with the Divine in order to tap into Divine inspiration and guidance. Nevertheless, every time the project nears completion something goes wrong. Eventually, the individual takes a moment to close her eyes in order to visualize the project's successful completion. In doing so, via a flash of inspiration, the individual experiences an epiphany offering a solution to bypass a major obstacle blocking the task's completion. Later, on the way home from work, the individual sees several groundhogs and recognizes the animal as a messenger of intuition, the home, special projects, and the symbolic representation of a two-year cycle of change and transformation. Sure enough, upon returning home, the individual finds out a contractor has called back about work on a renovation project. She is ready for the future due to the sighting of the groundhog and its symbolic interpretation; the individual has the understanding that the project will soon be under way and calls a friend to cancel an expensive weekend out of town. Instead of opting for travel or a more affordable trip to the movies, the individual stays home to prepare for the renovation that will likely take a long time and prove costly. The individual prepares an evening meal, gives thanks to the Divine for her blessings and the food she is about to consume. With a final evening grounding meditation, she turns in for bed with a dream journal under her pillow. If she has a dream, she records it as soon as possible in the journal. She analyzes the dream during her waking hours for messages from the subconscious. The interpretation of messages received in dreams later enhances the individual's day-to-day existence.

While some may not share the beliefs of the Wiccan in the latter example, it is safe to suggest the individual's behavior is adaptive, not maladaptive. There is no distress caused by the individual's beliefs, and the only existing stress is the everyday stress in life everyone deals with differently. In fact, the Wiccan religion improves the individual's functioning and problem-solving abilities rather than impairing the individual's progress. The practitioner's Magickal understandings add a deeper layer of meaning to her life and further enhance her coping skills. As a matter of lifestyle differences, some may see her spiritual routines as inconvenient, too much work, or strange. However, akin to the routine of a violinist who practices for several hours each day to establish a routine and build skill, regular religious practices often prove beneficial and are not a matter of self-punishment or obsession. There is no inherent danger in religious practices tempered with moderation. They contribute to one's life experience; they do not cause the individual to psychologically shut down, lose contact with peers, or to jeopardize quality of work function or the ability to care for the self.

There are religions that promote the belief that to practice divination or to hold polytheistic beliefs jeopardizes the soul causing, in the mind of the non-Wiccan, a real form of spiritual danger. This is a subjective argument based on perspective alone and has no foundation in mental illness, its symptoms, or its diagnosis or treatment. This is not the same as assessing for danger caused by a mental illness. In contrast, if someone were truly in danger of harming themselves or others or presented suicidal or homicidal ideations, a professional would have a legal and moral obligation to intervene.

SPIRITS, DIVINE GUIDANCE, AND HALLUCINATIONS

Wiccans follow guidance from the God and Goddess, ancestors, and various spirit guides. Wiccans believe in the value of animal appearances in daily life, and in the symbolic value of dreams, Tarot card readings, and other forms of divination. The guidance Wiccans perceive is a means of navigating life's challenges and is also comforting; even in cases of omens or warnings, practitioners do not receive messages or communications which are in any way self-destructive or that command the harm or destruction of others or property. Wiccans do not confuse Divine communication with instructions to cause harm to the self, to others, or to property, and most Wiccans, having experienced spirit guidance, will confirm a higher-level energy being (deity or a spirit guide) *never* instructs someone to behave in a damaging, dangerous, or reckless manner. The voice that tells someone to tell their boss to go to hell and take off for Vegas without a drop of money in the bank and no job to return to after an impromptu trip is not coming from the God and Goddess or a spirit guide!

Most religions hold some belief in spirit/human interaction whether accessible by all or reserved for only highly initiated or chosen members. A negative, destructive, or fear-inducing voice is not a religious experience. The difference between guidance and hallucination is the fine line between constructive and de-constructive guidance. Even still, the line is sometimes blurred. For example, in some Eastern religions, practitioners of certain religious traditions undergo prolonged fasting in order to attain purification. One could argue this is potentially dangerous, but considering factors like the total level of cognitive and physical functioning, and the duration of the fasting, among other factors, helps determine whether the practice is dangerous or benign.

Wiccans sometimes hear or "intuit" guidance from the God and Goddess or spirit which intervenes in times when one may normally lose their focus or fall prey to strong emotions that misguide otherwise logical human instincts. This guidance has proven helpful in arriving at solutions that would not have surfaced strictly within the mundane world. Some would label the experience an acknowledgment of one's intuition and disregard it as not worthy of the same status as God and Goddess or spirit, but this, again, is a matter of perception and attribution within one's belief system.

A Note to All Occult Practitioners: If a practitioner hears a voice instructing the harm of the self or others, it is not a positive enlightening experience. The practitioner must therefore treat the situation with concern.

In some cases, when dealing with paranormal activity, a practitioner may experience activity associated with negative entities or spirits: This may be one reason behind hearing a voice offering harmful instruction. However, one should always look to mundane answers first before assuming anything is paranormal. Therefore, it is recommended that the practitioner first seek out professional counseling services to rule out the possibility of a mental illness.

In some instances, a counselor or psychiatrist may perceive a Wiccan's beliefs as bizarre or strange. When it comes to the diagnosis of mental illnesses, a professional may erroneously identify the behaviors of a Wiccan as indicative of a mental illness. It is important to note the individual must first present with a degree of dysfunction or distress if a mental health professional is going to consider behavioral symptoms characteristic of a psychotic disorder or mental illness.

It's important not to forget that society attempts, and often succeeds, at defining what is or is not acceptable. At one time in history, members of alternative religious or cultural groups, like Native Americans or other Aboriginal people worldwide for example, were marginalized and oppressed for their beliefs. Society, at one time, identified these groups as evil, savage, unintelligent, uncivilized, misguided, or crazy. Within relatively recent history, mental health professionals identified homosexuality as a mental illness until better understandings called for the elimination of such a diagnosis. The scope of error in society's definition of what is "normal," and society's response to groups of people who are different is wide, extending well beyond the scope of this book. Nevertheless, it is clear that although Wiccans and other Pagans may hold beliefs that others have trouble grasping as real: Such beliefs stem from a religious system with roots in Pre-Christian religions found all over the world. What's more, the beliefs Wiccans embrace are no more bizarre or psychotic to a practitioner of the Wiccan faith than the religious notions embraced by practitioners of any other religion. Such beliefs may include, but are not limited to messages from the Divine appearing in nature, the belief in the ability to heal the sick, reincarnation, interaction with Divine and semi-Divine beings, and the ability to call on the Divine to intervene and alter the course of current reality through the practice of prayer.

MAGICK VERSUS SELF-DELUSION

Rational thinking refers to the ability to interpret events accurately based on known reality. For Wiccans, spirit is as much a part of reality as the physical world. Magick calls for the interaction of spiritual and mundane principals to allow one's intent to alter the course of future events and to make changes in one's life. Rationality is a key ingredient in Magickal practices; in order to work Magick and to have it prove effective, the practitioner must attune to the evidence present in the situation and change desired. In other words, one must be keenly aware of various parts of a problem, and possible solutions that exist in the mundane world prior to resorting to Magick. To wander around oblivious and to hope Magick will bail a person out of problems without considering mundane resources and consequences is nothing short of self-delusion.

Through Magick, a Witch seeks a clear outcome or goal through the application of energies—primarily through the mind, but also with the assistance of corresponding herbs, colored candles, symbolic images, stones, or other tools. The Witch can raise energy during a spell working and send it out to the God, Goddess, and universe. It is a supercharged prayer with accessories in some cases, as opposed to a passive wish that one ponders but does not invest physical or spiritual energy into creating. Following a Magickal working, it is imperative the individual does everything possible to remain open to the manifestation of their outcome without trying too hard to control things. At the same time, the practitioner must make an effort to achieve the resolution sought.

Self-delusion, on the other hand, is a close cousin of superstition, and "magical thinking" is not the same thing as "thinking in Magickal terms." Magical thinking, when speaking in the terms of a mental illness, is a passive attempt to control reality by wishing and the process of attributing power to one's self without a basis in reality: This can result in saying a thing is so and pretending it is, even when all evidence exists to the contrary. It is akin to trying to run a car with no gas. Remember, Witches do not make things happen with Magick without powerful intent and universal assistance; Witches draw on the spiritual energy of the universe and this interaction causes things to happen based upon the intent of the practitioner. The human alone is the "car" or vehicle, which cannot run without "fuel" or universal assistance. In contrast, "thinking in Magickal terms" occurs when a practitioner's thoughts and actions support a focused, intent-based, spiritually charged ritual or spell working.

If it seems odd to think that a Magickal action like burning a sage stick can cleanse a home of negative energy, consider the understanding of transubstantiation in a Christian context: The symbolic power used to transform bread, grape juice, or wine into a sacrament. It is the ritual intent and energy endowing the latter objects with meaning beyond their mundane purpose, thereby causing their mystical transformation into sacred objects.

Yet another instance of pop culture taking an occult practice and watering it down for easy consumption is the recent emphasis on the misunderstood practice of better living through affirmation. Words do have power. The problem arises when people believe that just making a statement or reading a phrase in their mind will transform their lives. This is not Magick; it is mental thigh cream. Magick is simple, but not always easy: It requires energy, work, commitment, and discipline. Magickal workings are never a passive process. Even mentally stable individuals are sometimes guilty of wishful-thinking and the self-delusion it brings.

Imagine a woman who affirms mentally how successful she will be because she is committed to her diet. Silently in her mind, she repeats how great she will look and how good she will feel if she remains committed to the diet. She visualizes how she wants to look after losing all the weight she wants to lose. She does well with her affirmations and visualizations until a fast food worker calls her to the counter to order her food, and she orders a fattening meal. The techniques of affirmation and visualization are not at fault here; it is the lack of follow through, *will* power, or the belief that a person can dream big, enact the opposite in one's mundane reality, and still somehow achieve the desired result. Magick requires one's mental and spiritual intentions match their mundane actions, and without such an alignment, a practitioner weakens Magickal workings.

Consider the following: Everything is energy. If a Witch invests an hour in a ritual to cleanse themselves and their home of negative energy, that's great. But if the individual then invests twelve hours in verbally putting down everyone and everything around them, acting in negative ways, lying or committing other negative or destructive acts, they are lowering (negating) the positive energy he or she worked so hard to raise. Unfortunately, people confuse this type of self-delusion with the practice of Magick, and then respond to people who successfully practice Magick as if they are missing the "mystical secret" or a few important pieces of hardware.

WICCAN AND TROUBLED

Like any human being, practitioners of Wicca may face their own challenges. These tests and obstacles may manifest in mental or physical illnesses. It is tragic that in the 1990s one could occasionally find news stories with headlines such as "Teen Witch Kills Self." As of yet, the authors of this text have not heard of a suicide reported in a more mainstream faith, which a reporter would have the audacity to attribute to the individual's religion. As Wicca grows in popularity, it will become more evident that people who practice Wicca are also people who experience the same types of problems as the rest of the world. Drug abuse, mental illness, domestic violence: These social and personal problems are not offshoots of being a Witch. It is sad when an individual in crisis seeks out professional help that he or she cannot always readily expect an open acceptance of what could be one of their assets: a strong faith and lasting spirituality. More often than not, mental health professionals disregard, avoid, judge, or skeptically view, if not outright blame a Wiccan's faith for a Witch's entanglement in some life problem.

To its credit, the human service fields are beginning to recognize the value of engaging people's cultural and religious beliefs in order to assist them in finding hope and solving problems. The new trend in "cultural competency" requires training in social work fields so an encounter with someone of a different background will facilitate a dialog about what is important to the person, without the judgment or dis-easing of someone's religious beliefs. Mental health professionals are slowly figuring out that a person's faith is not something that one avoids or corrects in a clinical setting. Qualified professionals are now learning to ask about religious beliefs and sources of faith and inspiration. This then allows the individual to access a client's spirituality as a resource to help in the healing of the individual.

Educational resources are now beginning to teach that diagnosing Wiccan beliefs or beliefs in the reality of Magick as a form of psychosis is not an option, and that it is better for a worker or counselor who is not familiar with the culture to ask the client for an explanation about his or her beliefs. It is hoped in the near future, the notion of blaming tragedy such as suicide or other traumatic life events on the individual's religion or beliefs in Magick will cease entirely and the field will widely-recognize a person's psychological crises does not necessarily stem from their religious choices. A person's religious views, if different than those views held by the majority of the population, doesn't mean the person is misled and in need of being saved or corrected.

WITCHES BEHAVING BADLY

The last decade has been groundbreaking for the growing acceptance of Wicca in cultures worldwide. From a time when the word "Wicca" was "Greek" to a non-practitioner of the faith to the present day explosion of interest in the faith system, this shift in awareness has brought notoriety. In truth, the resemblance of the characters to followers of the Old Religion in contemporary films is often more in name than in deed. At the same time, modern movies about Witchcraft tend to exemplify a real issue in the resurgence of The Craft: the misuse of the practices of Magick and other tenets of Wicca for personal gain, negative attention, or shock value.

Some say a little information is a dangerous thing; this is particularly true when it comes to a little bit of knowledge of the occult and Magickal practices. It is normal for a person to experience excitement at the thought of all of the possibilities open to the mind, body, and spirit when one has engaged all the senses. When the sky is the limit, what person can resist the temptation to use Magick to win a lover, gain power, money, or seek revenge? These temptations are so strong they seemingly occur in every sci-fi/fantasy story ever written. However, these stories usually end with negative consequences as a result.

Wicca is a religion, but humans are the vessel for these spiritual principles. Countless times practitioners have been angered, wanted a quick solution to a problem, or thought how nice it would be if someone would rekindle an old relationship. Why shouldn't a practitioner use Magick to get his or her way in a specific situation? The answer is simple, because it is not the Wiccan way. Wiccans believe in karma and consequences for all actions, mundane or Magickal. Wiccans strive for adherence to the rede: "An it harm none, do what you will," although this adherence is an ideal, to be entirely honest, as human beings, everyone is fallible, and the reality is that sometimes Wiccans can fall short of their own higher, guiding principle. Nevertheless, Wiccans never cease striving to adhere to the "harm none," rule.

In The Craft, it is widely understood that Magick works, and the intentions set forth in Magick shape real outcomes. The practitioner does not take this power lightly. For Witches misusing Magick, many practitioners belief a threefold return awaits; in other words, in this lifetime or in others, the consequences of one's actions return on him or her, times three. When a practitioner uses Magick to harm, then harm returns onto the practitioner. It is not a bargain worth taking as any serious practitioner will instruct. Still, curiosity or poor coping skills will sometimes lead people to make mistakes with Magick. People do tempt bad karma by seeking selfish, vindictive, or spiteful goals via Magick and their actions, and this can result in outcomes that bring negativity into their life. When a practitioner wants to use Magick to get revenge, they shouldn't be surprised if the ache or pain inflicted on an enemy returns, threefold. The same principles apply to acts of selfishness or greed. In general, it only takes one or two episodes of Magickal misuse for a misguided practitioner to either get the karmic message or give up on the occult altogether, sometimes citing the "dangers" inherent in delving into the mysteries. Sometimes these dangers are nothing more than the karmic consequences of misusing Magick.

WHAT RESPONSIBLE WITCHES DON'T DO

Magick done to show off, validate one's insecurities, or respond to a demand to prove the existence of Magick is a waste of time. Whether the act of showing off one's Magickal skills in an effort to prove the validity of Magick or to elevate one's ego, such actions are not serving a real purpose. The shallow use of a sacred practice would be like asking a nun or priest to "make something happen" by praying in order to satisfy one's curiosity. Using Magick to change a skeptic's mind is manipulating one's free will to disbelieve. Magick is not a competitive sport and use of the mysteries in order to prove one's self is ego-based, not spiritual. Even if it appears the ritual was a success, the act of succumbing to the ego to show off lowers one's energy vibrations, creates karmic residue, and will return to remind the practitioner of their mistake even if it takes a while for repercussions to unfold.

LOVE, GREED, POWER, REVENGE

If Magick really works, why not have it all? Magick is a neutral practice. It is the process of applying mental/spiritual energy to effect change in the material world. It is possible to use Magick to obtain whatever one desires, but to do so is not advisable. Love spells are popular, but most times unethical. To seek to manipulate someone's attraction or interest as a partner is to interfere with their free will. Can it work? Yes, but at the cost of robbing someone of their choice and robbing the practitioner of a partner who would seek them out without the use of Magick as a lure.

Can Magick link someone with money and material goods? Yes, it can. Used carelessly however, a person's karma will reflect the buildup of greed or ego-driven desires. Trying to make ends meet when survival is at stake is one thing, but using Magick to propel one's finances ahead is a double-edged sword. Consider a person landing a job with the help of a Magickal ritual, only to find out the job is not what the person is best suited for, and a better opportunity was lost in the process. When it comes to mundane issues, it is better to do the footwork through traditional means, and to only resort to Magick to assist one's mundane work if necessary. Would a person really want a job (lover, friend, business opportunity) because of Magick? In general, Wiccans may use Magick to protect their finances, to bring love into their lives, and to help connect with business opportunities, but should always use Magick with a spiritual sense of priorities. If a new job is a matter of survival in a tough economy or if increasing assets is crucial to basic needs, it is more acceptable to use Magick sparingly and with moderation than it is to use Magickal practices in an effort to become the next millionaire. The saying "be careful what you ask for" applies, and the universe has a way of reminding a practitioner of their priorities. For example, the practitioner might gain massive wealth through Magickal workings, albeit with a catch.

When it comes to attaining power in a situation, Magick is better when the practitioner uses it as a tool to develop confidence and self-control, mastery of one's self, and an understanding of one's limitations. The first ambition of a Witch is to "know thyself," this also means fully understanding one's own motivations for performing spells and for working with Magick. If the practitioner grasps an understanding of internal motivations, he or she can avoid Magickal chaos and the severe repercussions for unethical actions. Using Magick to obtain power over another is a good way to attract bad karma. In doing this, one seeks to use Magick in a manipulative manner in social situations.

Revenge or spite is a powerful force. Using Magick to seek revenge or to be spiteful is negative and destructive. The karmic consequences are clear. Use Magick to direct negativity toward an individual, whether they seemingly "deserve" it or not, and negativity in one form or another will return onto the sender, times three. Use Magick to in any way harm, curse, or take something away from another, one may as well picture oneself on the receiving end, because the results will play out in the practitioner's life as well, many-fold, and carry heavy consequences.

Magick can be used for protection if need be, but deflecting negative is not the same as deliberately sending negative to another, no matter how much their behavior or attitude may seem to warrant it. This is a tough lesson for many people because in daily life it seems that many people get away with doing wrong. It would be great to have the authority to put ignorance in its place, but this is the God and Goddess's job, not that of the individual.

These days, it is hard to avoid victimization in some way, great or small, by those who are not concerned with the rights and wellbeing of others. For Wiccans, resorting to Magick to bring revenge on another has never been an option. Wiccans have a belief in a universal justice consisting of karma, doled out by the God and Goddess and while it may be difficult, Wiccans strive to remember at all times it is not one's responsibility to act as Magickally empowered vigilantes on earth. A Witch can use Magick to ask the God and Goddess to bring justice to a person if they are harmed or wronged, but this is not the same as directing negativity to a person. It is up to the God and Goddess to decide what is just in a matter, not to humans reacting to strong, negative-based emotions. This is the ideal, but it would be deceiving to say practitioners of The Craft never slip and let the lure of emotion lead to bad judgment in Magickal workings. Rest assured however, the God and Goddess, through karmic repercussions, reminds them swiftly of why Magickal practitioners are not supposed to let their negative, out-of-control emotions be the determining factor in how Magick is used.

Although Wiccans don't follow the Ten Commandments, they do have a system of laws and consequences guiding their practices. As open as The Craft may seem to outsiders, it is anything but a free-for-all when it comes to Magick and conduct. Sadly, there are times when even Witches, being fallible humans, succumb to the temptation to misuse their learning or to forget it altogether and act on emotion alone. This is an atomic bomb in the realm of Magick. When these individuals find themselves in the midst of self-induced chaos, all attention seems to first go to their religion, second, to excuses made for their behavior, and last, on the person's inherent loss of control and misbehavior.

It seems society reacts to outrageous behavior committed by self-proclaimed Wiccans as if their actions exemplify a Witch, rather than doing the research first to establish the incidents present an example of an immoral person. The trend is to draw attention to the religious affiliation and "evidence" that the crime was religiously motivated, even if inaccurate, and then incorporate facts from knowledgeable Wiccans or members of the community after the damage has been done. It is a shoot first, research and apologize later approach that contributes to the misunderstandings Wiccans face every day.

Recently in 2010, in the Southwestern United States, a self-titled "Witch" allegedly stabbed her significant other in what she called a "sacrifice." The timing coincided with Spring Equinox, erroneously labeled Beltane by the local authorities.[1] The woman allegedly carried her athame around with her and used the knife to commit the crime. Misunderstandings about the Wiccan religion resulted in many errors early on in the investigation and the reporting of this particular incident. Fortunately, an outpouring of protests from the Wiccan community (including the authors of this book) presented the facts and those who perpetuated the misinformation clarified the situation. Wiccans spoke up locally and nationwide to present the facts about Wiccan practices, resulting in new media reports. As any lawyer will advise however, once someone shares information as "evidence" in a trial, no amount of direction from a judge to disregard it will erase the misinformation, thereby resulting in an instantaneous bias formation in the minds of jurors. Likewise, no amount of factual counter argument in the press will truly correct the damage done by media-hyped, sensationalized campaigns.

It is of the opinion of the authors of this text that if this woman had studied Wicca, her actions in stabbing her partner were not related to any tenets of Witchcraft, and her actions were driven by some motivation only she will ever know. The only sacrifice demanded in The Craft is that of time and energy. The Wiccan Rede is made clear even to novices. As mentioned earlier, the ritual knife, an athame, identified as a "Wiccan dagger" in the press, is not for the purposes of bloodletting. Contact with blood renders it a tool ineffective in Magickal practices. Once corrupted, the tool must then be disposed of and a new athame used. An athame is a tool used for the purposes of extending one's Magickal energies, for visualization purposes during ritual, and it is highly unlikely one will find the average Wiccan carrying one around. Usually, the athame remains on the altar for safekeeping. Always remember killing plays no part of being Wiccan and any alleged Wiccan that cites the practice of Witchcraft as the reason behind malicious acts is nothing more than a misinformed individual who does not fully understand the tenets of Wicca, or a person who has never really legitimately participated in Wiccan practices at all.

A different scenario emerged when members of a Midwestern Christian fundamentalist commune opened fire on a funeral rite in 2010. Although the press covered the story with an inclusion of the shooters' participation in an extremist commune, the portrayal was absent of an emphasis on the assailants' religion. Thus, the press portrayed the assailants' actions as the exception to the rule and not to a representation of all Christians.[2] Imagine how the understanding and acceptance of Wiccans would differ if the media extended the same clarification when individuals act on their emotions and disturbances and not on their spiritual ethics.

Another recent example emerged in 2010, when a man allegedly killed his girlfriend, and his explanation for doing so upon his arrest was that his girlfriend had broken a blood oath: allegedly a Wiccan pledge binding the couple.[3] Witches do make oaths to the Gods and Goddesses but these are statements of devotion and intent and do not involve blood spilling. Wiccans are capable of pledging their fealty to chosen deities through beautiful initiation rituals and dedications or through prayers without resorting to extremist self-mutilation, the mutilation of others, or attention-seeking measures. When a Wiccan practitioner makes an oath to the Divine; it is not a tool to manipulate or control others. To what extent this person was involved in Wicca is unknown, if at all. The man apparently turned to his self-proclaimed faith as a scapegoat in order to try to avoid the consequences for his actions or to try to offer a poor justification for his behaviors, but his true beliefs toward women are apparent in his past actions. Logically, one cannot hold the God and Goddess in high regard and abuse one's partner at the same time, no matter what religion they profess to follow. Some covens turn away potential students who cannot manage to break the cycle of abusing women or people in action or words: To behave abusively expresses the individual's lack of regard for people and therefore translates into a lack of respect for the Feminine and Masculine Divine.

Another type of common media sensation often occurs right around Samhain or Halloween. It seems to be a practice of picking up any obscure incident and cashing in on the timing; papers love to attribute crimes of various kinds, from vandalism to robbery, to Witchcraft. There are different people who upset gravesites, spray paint graffiti, or who mistreat animals. In some cases, the disturbed individuals or attention seekers act out and do foolish things. Others like to dabble with little understanding or reverence for the Magickal Arts or they love to show off using some erroneous occult knowledge to shock the authorities in their lives. This lends to the poorly developed understandings society holds about Witchcraft. An example of this all too common sensationalizing of pseudo-occult crimes occurred in New England 2007. A grave was disturbed, robbed, and the local authorities attributed the crime to Witches. Local Wiccans spoke out to correct the issue, and a local, non-Wiccan shop owner, set the record straight by supplying the media more information on Wicca.[5] In such cases, even if authorities issue an apology after the fact, the apology comes too late, only after the formation of public opinion.

An important note: It is not fair, but necessary, that Wiccans have to hold themselves to a high standard of conduct and ethics. Wiccans are human and make mistakes. They can succumb to emotions, get angry, and let their impulses get the better of them. To the extent that a practitioner is able, one *must* be cognizant of the damage bad choices potentially have on the reputation of the entire Wiccan faith. It is an unfair double standard, but it exists nonetheless. Practitioners must bear in mind that society will often perceive the practitioner's misguided deeds as the result of the Witch's religious preferences, not their individual problems or foolish mistakes. With this in mind, Wiccans, especially young, still-maturing individuals and neophyte practitioners, take heed.

IT'S ESBAT

DO YOU KNOW WHERE YOUR KIDS ARE?

Wiccan adults often grew from Wiccan teens. The authors of this book understand from experience how hard it can be to discover Wicca as a youth and have to educate one's self along the way, sometimes the hard way. Unlike their Judeo-Muslim-Christian-Hindu peers and peers with other religious orientations, one's family seldom introduces practitioners to The Craft. It is also not likely to be one's original religious curriculum within the context of a private school, religious education program, or other community-based organization. For most of us, an understanding of Wicca develops first by reading the works of others and exploring, as a solitary or with equally novice practitioners, the complexities of this faith. Being a teenager is difficult enough, but trying to navigate close to a largely misunderstood faith with little outside guidance, can add confusion to an already turbulent time in one's life. Without external guidance, reminders of ethics, and the availability of knowledgeable individuals to answer questions from experience, teen Wiccans face the difficulty of self-instruction and trial and error practice. Is it any wonder they sometimes fall prey to poor judgment and act foolishly, reaping self-imposed negative consequences, and negatively influencing the public view of the religion?

Consider with a grain of consecrated sea-salt the young, novice practitioner who has learned the theory of their religion through books alone. The instruction is helpful but their questions about applying the techniques and practices to their daily life go unanswered because there are no adults or knowledgeable individuals in their life who understand the philosophy they are learning. Perhaps they hide their interest from family, or perhaps the family is supportive but lacks the knowledge to guide them in their undertaking. Perhaps they search for answers to their questions on the Internet, only to find a plethora of mixed reports, conflicting advice, and personal opinions from people they have never met. These people offering advice could even be less experienced than the teen, or have an ulterior motive in sharing the information that they share. Thus, novice practitioners can wind up confused, misguided, and unable to separate the positive influences from the nonsense.

TEENS AND WICCA

Hopefully, open-minded adults close to a youth with interests in Wicca will explore with the teen, as a co-pilot and guide. One should help provide a grounded sounding board for information that may raise a red flag. At the same time, suspend judgment and consider the validity of a culture even if it is new or unfamiliar; an adult should help the teen develop the discernment to decipher which information seems positive, and which seems harmful. Seek the expertise of local practitioners when questions arise. Even if the local Priest/Priestess does not mentor the youth individually, shop owners or local practitioners many times want to advise novices and are happy to answer questions or suggest helpful books or websites. This will help sort out the best information in a world of information overload. Of course, this hope is idealistic. Many Wiccans accept that parents have a right to discourage their children from exploring things they do not approve of, and many Wiccan leaders ask youths to refrain from using their interest in The Craft in a deceitful, disrespectful way. Many Wiccans do not condone studying in secret or without parental consent. The question remains: How can a person honor a God and Goddess if they cannot honor their own parent's instructive guidance?

As a teen, not being able to study Wicca because it is against your parent's values and you do not have parental consent to do so may prove disappointing. However, if the Wiccan path is the ideal path for an individual, he or she will find a way to pursue the religious course as an adult. In the parent's home, the teen is subject to the parent's rules and judgment. The God and Goddess have been around for centuries, and will not disappear by the time a person turns eighteen — our coven does not teach minors without the consent of their parent(s). Many spiritual leaders turn away youth who express an interest in Wicca, but also plan to hide it from their parents. Hiding one's practices is unethical and potentially dangerous to family relationships. If someone

A youthful Witch, Earth Goddess, and a Sun and Moon plaque.

is sincere in his or her desire to become a Witch, the God and Goddess will be waiting for them to be of age when they can then make their own choices with maturity and without deceit.

Consider the time spent developing through your teens as a time for practicing tolerance and patience, both necessary to practicing Magick and far more important than getting a head start on practicing spells and building up a grimoire. Meanwhile, if the reader is an adult reading this book and he or she knows of a young person interested in Wicca, seek to understand the religious system before discouraging them. Enlist the help of local adult practitioners. Who knows, their advice may even result in a child making positive life changes, illustrating a propensity for greater responsibility, and one might even experience the Magickal moment when after arriving home from work one finds the child has finished their homework and the dishes are done! Okay, maybe expecting the child to do the homework and dishes without continual prompting is *a little bit* of a stretch. Who knows, their advice may even result in a child making positive life changes, illustrating a propensity for greater responsibility, and one might even experience the Magickal moment when after arriving home from work one finds the child has finished their homework and the dishes are done!

HANDLING RELIGIOUS INTOLERANCE AND DISCRIMINATION

"Laws alone cannot secure freedom of expression; in order that every man presents his views without penalty there must be spirit of tolerance in the entire population."

~Albert Einstein

There are different ways for Wiccans to deal with religious intolerance and discrimination. How a practitioner handles a situation is determined on a case-by-case basis. The practitioner will need to give careful consideration as to whether or not to devote energy to dealing with intolerant and discriminatory issues. On occasion, the act of feeding energy to a situation results in the poisoning of the practitioner's life, whereas some issues demand an appropriate, responsive action.

If it is possible to do so, the practitioner will want to consider walking away from the issue, especially if the problem involves an attempt to alter a "fixed mindset." In some cases, no amount of arguing or debate will change the mind of another, and in the end, a person has the right to belief as he or she chooses. A practitioner may not necessarily like what another believes, but an attempt to alter such a belief is often futile. Sometimes agreeing to disagree is the best response that a person can have to an uncomfortable, religiously intolerant situation.

If the practitioner feels their First Amendment rights are violated, or if the practitioner feels they are a victim of discrimination on the job or in a school setting based on his or her religion, it is a good time to contact an attorney or to contact the American Civil Liberties Union (ACLU). If the situation involves a hate crime or any acts of violence, the practitioner should contact local authorities immediately. A Witch should never become a vigilante, and acts of religious intolerance and discrimination should never involve revenge, violence, or aggressive retaliation.

No matter what the situation is, the practitioner should never lower him or herself by mirroring the attitude of the individual or organization acting in an intolerant or discriminatory nature. Aggressive rebuttals can seemingly indicate a lack in confidence about one's beliefs. In addition, when the practitioner is aggressive in response to intolerant or discriminatory acts, he or she may end up supporting the arguments set forth by the perceived aggressor. There is a difference between assertiveness and aggression.

On a final note: There are some instances where it is best to keep silent; there are some occasions when keeping silent isn't an ideal option. When a Wiccan has the unique opportunity to educate others about the faith system, the practitioner should seize the opening. The more Wiccans who speak out about the religion and who share information about Wiccan traditions, beliefs, and practices, the more people will have the chance to learn about the true nature of Wiccan practices. Through education, religious tolerance can result, even if it is through the act of educating one person at a time. However, when sharing information about Wicca, a practitioner must remember sharing information is not converting someone to the Wiccan faith. If Wiccans begin to speak out more often, they can become a strong vocal force: one that can work in unison in the form of education and outreach. In turn, little by little, misconceptions about Wicca may radically diminish, and Wiccans may eventually promote a greater spirit of religious tolerance as a result.

GLOSSARY

ALTAR
A table, rock, tree stump, or other flat surface that is consecrated and used as an area for holding sacred objects, statues, and tools. The practitioner uses an altar for esoteric purposes only, and is a place where one can pay honor to the Divine, leave offerings, and keep ritual tools safe.

ASTRAL PROJECTION
A practice that involves the use of a trance, dream, or meditative state so a practitioner can explore and work in alternative realms. The use of an altered form of awareness to have an "out of body" experience through the separation of one's spiritual body from one's physical body so that one can move and work in realms entirely non-physical.

ATHAME
A ritual knife used for the process of casting Magick circles or for use in spell casting; a dagger is not for mundane purposes or for the purposes of bloodletting.

BANISHING
A banishing is a ritual or spell involving the casting out of negative entities or spirits. It is equivalent to a Christian exorcism.

BAPHOMET
The Goat God: a deity depicted with the body of a man and a goat head.

BURNING TIMES
The Burning Times refers to the torture and extermination of alleged Witches, particularly prevalent during the fifteenth and eighteenth centuries. The number of people who died during the time as a result varies widely

from 50,000 to 9 million. The term is somewhat misleading, suggesting the burning at the stake of all accused Witches. Some of the accused died at the stake, whereas many of them were tortured, tried, imprisoned, hanged, or killed via alternative means.

CHROMOTHERAPY
The utilization of light and color for the purposes of healing; chromotherapy involves the understanding that colors have various frequencies, all that can be used for the purposes of healing the body through continual, repetitious or prolonged exposure to the color frequencies.

CLAIRAUDIENCE
The innate ability to hear things/spirits without the use of one's physical ears; clairaudience is considered a "psychic" ability that allows the individual to psychically hear things beyond average human perception.

CLAIRGUSTANCE
The innate ability to taste something without the actual physical consumption of foods; clairaugustance is considered a "psychic" ability that allows the individual to psychically taste things beyond average human perception.

CLAIROLFACTORY
The innate ability to smell scents or odors without the use of one's physical nose; clairolfactory is considered a "psychic" ability that allows the individual to psychically smell things beyond average human perception.

CLAIRSENTIENCE
The innate ability to feel or sense someone or something without the use of one's physical senses; clairsentience is considered a "psychic" ability that allows the individual to psychically detect or sense beyond average human perception.

CLAIRVOYANCE
The innate ability to see someone, something, or an event without the use of one's physical eyes; clairvoyance is considered a "psychic" ability that allows the individual to psychically see, witness, or visualize someone, something, or events beyond average human perception.

CLEARING
See *Banishing*.

COVEN
A gathering of Witches: A group of Witches consisting of three or more individuals who celebrate the sabbats (rituals celebrating the seasons), esbats (full moon rituals), perform Magickal workings together, and serve as a spiritual support system for one another.

COVENANT

A covenant is the promise between the Christian God and humankind, or the term covenant refers to a contract or an agreement.

CROSSING

A crossing is a special ritual, a rite of passage, used to help a deceased spirit "cross over" to other realms so the spirit may continue his or her spirit journey and evolution. A crossing is also an event that allows friends and family members to say their final good-byes to the departed, to honor the departed, and to share fond memories about their friends and loved ones.

CULT

In an archaic sense, a cult is a group that venerates one or more deities; in a modern sense, the word means as a group that holds atypical, disturbing, and potentially harmful beliefs.

DEITIES

Deities are Gods and Goddesses that are depictions and understandings of the single Divine being.

DIVINATION

Divination is the use of various means to predict or foresee upcoming challenges, changes, obstacles, or events. The practice often involves the use of tools including but not limited to crystal balls, tarot cards, pendulum boards, runes, the I Ching, and many other divinatory methods.

DREAM INTERPRETATION

The remembrance of dreams and its symbols; the symbols are later interpreted by the dreamer in order to draw insight from the subconscious.

DREAM JOURNAL

A journal, notebook, or stored recordings of one's dreams for the purposes of future interpretation.

ELEMENTALS

Nature spirits or creatures of the four elements: Air, Fire, Water, and Earth. These nature spirits include gnomes, salamanders, sylphs, and undines.

ENERGY MEDICINE

A form of holistic healing that involves the act of rebalancing one's bodily energies in order to deal with a variety of illnesses as well as to promote the well-being of the individual.

ENTRY RITE

A rite used by Witches before or after a circle casting that permits entry of practitioners into a sacred area.

ESBAT
Monthly celebrations and rituals held on the night of the full moon; a gathering where practitioners recognize, acknowledge, and revere the Goddess and God aspects of the Divine, often with a primary focus on the Goddess aspect.

EXORCISM
An exorcism is the act of forcing out negative spirits, demons, or lower level entities from a person, place, or thing.

FAMILIAR
A familiar is an animal sharing a loving, spiritual bond with a Witch. A familiar can lend its energies to Magickal workings.

GARDNERIAN WICCA
A tradition of Wicca started in the 1950s established by Gerald Gardner. Gardner is one of the founding fathers of the Wiccan movement, but Gardnerian Wicca is one of many traditions within the Wiccan faith system.

HANDFASTING
A marriage rite performed by a High Priest, High Priestess, Priestess, or Priest.

HEREDITARY WITCH
An individual born into a family of Witches and raised as a Witch who continues practicing Witchcraft into adulthood is a hereditary Witch.

HEXES
A curse or negative spell empowered by negative intentions and associated with the desire for a negative outcome.

KARMA
A cause/effect principle where a person's actions are balanced by the notion that positive actions are rewarded by the Divine or universe, and negative actions are repaid unto the individual with equivalent negativity.

LOVE SPELLS
Magickal workings cast for bringing love into one's life or for causing the will of another to change and turn the individual's affections toward the practitioner or the person requesting the performance of the spell.

MAGIC
A term used to refer to magic for entertainment purposes, trickery, and sleight of hand practices. This term is different from that used to describe occult practices.

MAGICK CIRCLE
A circle cast before spell workings or rituals that creates a protective boundary. The circle is cast by a practitioner and creates a space considered "between the mundane world and other worldly or Magickal realms," and one that makes the area sacred and safe for Magickal practices.

MAGICK
The term used to describe occult practices and Magick in relation to witchcraft.

NECROMANCY
Necromancy is the practice of communicating with deceased spirits for the purposes of divination.

NEW AGE
A term used to describe an enlightened mode of understanding; it encompasses a variety of religions, and it describes a historical movement as well as a movement away from widely accepted Western religious ideals toward the acceptance of unconventional theologies and ideologies from various cultures.

OCCULT
The word *occult* means "secret, concealed, or hidden" knowledge. Learning about the occult is the act of studying things defined as paranormal, supernatural, and spiritual and the gaining of hidden or secret knowledge from such studies.

OUIJA BOARDS
Boards containing letters, numbers, and words, used to communicate with the deceased and other entities. Many practitioners frown upon the use of the board because person might end up connecting with something that he or she might not want to connect with and the individual may find it next to impossible to break contact.

OUT OF BODY EXPERIENCE
An out-of-body-experience is the separation of the soul from one's physical body in the absence of a physical death. The soul then explores other worldly realms via astral projection while remaining connected to the body.

PAGAN
The term represents a member of society following "the old ways," some form of "earth-based" religion, or individuals that do not conform to a society's major religions; a term also used to refer to a polytheist whose practice is centered on the earth and nature.

PALMISTRY
Palmistry is the practice of examining the characteristics of a person's hands, fingers, fingertips, and wrists to make predictive determinations about the individual's life.

PENTACLE
A five-pointed star with a single point facing upward that is fully enclosed within a circle. All of the points on the star connect to the outer, circular ring.

PENTAGRAM
A five-pointed star with two points facing upward enclosed inside a circle with all of the points touching the outer circular ring.

PSYCHIC
Abilities to cause action or to perceive things; the ability is believe to be stemming from one's mind instead of from physical actions. Wiccans view psychic abilities as innate to all people. Psychic abilities are not supernatural.

PSYCHOMETRY
Psychometry is the ability to hold an object and to derive insight into the object's owner, events, situations, or the history of the object through psychic means.

REFLEXOLOGY
A form of holistic healing wherein the practitioner purposefully applies pressure or massages various areas of the feet believed to stimulate and regulate other areas of the human body.

REIKI
A form of natural healing used to manipulate, stimulate, and correct bodily energies or bodily imbalances; a reliance on universal energies to heal through the hands via the process of channeling such energies.

REINCARNATION
Reincarnation is the belief that when someone dies they enter into another body and begin the life process over again. The belief is coupled with the understanding that in every life the soul has a special purpose, lessons to learn, and that the individual chooses the lessons to be mastered before his or her next incarnation.

RITUAL
A ritual is a religious, ceremonial observation, and celebration.

RULE OF THREE
See Three-Fold Law.

SABBAT
One of the eight high holy days in the Wiccan religion, sabbats are days of celebration marked by certain astronomical alignments or by specific times of the year.

SALEM WITCH TRIALS
The time occurring in the early 1690s where people were accused of Witchcraft, tried, and hanged. One victim was pressed to death after being convicted. The trials did not occur in modern-day Salem. Instead, they occurred in Salem Village, now known as Danvers, Massachusetts.

SATAN
Satan is primarily a Judeo-Christian concept; the adversary of God; an angelic being, in some literature, that is fallen and one that defied God. In doing so, Satan became the epitome of evil and is believed to encourage, to promote, and to cause evil acts on the earthly plane. Wiccans do not believe in Satan.

SATANIST
In conservative Satanic practices, a Satanist is a person who pays reverence to and serves Satan, viewing Satan as a God. In other cases, a Satanist may identify themselves as an individual that does not revere Satan, but that is in opposition of all creeds and religious systems.

SCRYING
Scrying is the practice of using various divinatory tools including crystal balls, candles, fire, or water to perceive future events, upcoming challenges, obstacles, or hidden information.

SEANCE
A séance is gathering of individuals with the intent of connecting with a deceased spirit or entity, often involving the practice of channeling.

SEX MAGICK
A working that involves physical and spiritual union of two people through sex; the mingling of the two auras of the people creating powerful sexual energies; the energies then used for a desired result. It is also a representation of the Divine union between the Goddess and the God: the Great Rite.

SIN
A transgression of some kind that breaches the religious principles established by the Judeo-Christian God: an action that is considered punishable by the same God. Wiccans do not believe in the concept of sin.

SKYCLAD
The practice of performing ritual working in the absence of clothing; this practice is performed by some practitioners as an indication of the freedom

that the practitioners have from the mundane world and its myriad limitations. Not all Wiccans perform rites skyclad.

SOLITARY WITCH
A practitioner who chooses to practice The Craft without participating in a coven or in the absence of other practitioners.

SPELLS
A Magickal working comprised of specific words, actions, and Magickal correspondences, all aimed at generating a desired result; spells are backed by the powerful intent of the practitioner.

SPIRIT COMMUNICATION
The act of communicating with deceased spirits or entities through various means including esoteric, psychic, and scientific means.

SWORD
A sword is a Magickal tool used in rituals for circle casting and other ritual purposes.

TAROT
A deck of 78 cards consisting of a major and minor arcana used for divination; a variety of card layouts is used for forecasting the future.

THREE-FOLD LAW
The basic understanding that whatever a person does comes back to the individual times three. The belief that one's intentions and actions are always balanced through a form of universal justice.

VISUALIZATION
The practice of developing and forming images or pictures in the mind; this practice is used in Magickal workings as well as during meditative practices.

WARLOCK
Someone that acts vengefully, creates disorder or chaos, uses deceit in Magickal practices. One considered "a traitor" of a particular faith.

WHEEL OF THE YEAR
The continual changing of the seasons marked by Wiccan sabbats.

WICCA
A legal and valid religion: one that serves as a guideline for a way of living one's life; a faith system involving a reverence of several deities, unified with monistic views, the reverence of nature, and the recognition of the Divine in all things.

WICCAN REDE
A harm none philosophy, one that all Wiccans aspire to in every instance: a moral and religious guideline.

WICCAN
A Wiccan is practitioner of the Magickal Arts within the context of a religion; a Witch following the philosophies of Wicca.

WICCANING
A Wiccaning is a rite of passage used when parents decide to request protection from the God and Goddess for a child.

WITCH HUNTS
A biased, unwavering, prejudice campaign against individuals accused of Witchcraft or individuals that practice Witchcraft. Witch hunts result in religious intolerance, violent hate crimes, and in many cases can result in the injury or death of the accused.

WITCH
The term Witch has myriad meanings; in a Wiccan sense, it is a person who practices the Magickal Arts. A wise person, a prophet, seer, and magician, one skilled in the art of sorcery, and one capable of consecration, divination, and enchantment. One who seeks to perceive new, esoteric, and mundane understandings and to learn and apply what he or she learns via observation. A Magickal practitioner with the ability to "bend one's self" via the process of bending or focusing their will and energies to create outward manifestations of their desires in the mundane world; the "bending of one's self," can also be extended to the notion of reaching beyond the physical plane to planes wholly spiritual and working within astral realms.

WITCHCRAFT
The application of esoteric, occult, and mundane knowledge, gained via study and experience, with strength, wisdom, and carefully honed skill. The use of Magickal practices in the mundane world.

RESOURCES

RECOMMENDED READING

Andrews, Ted. *Animal Speak: The Spiritual & Magical Powers of Creatures Great & Small*, Llewellyn Publications, St. Paul, Minnesota 1996.
A book exploring the messages that animals deliver and explains how to interpret such signs.

Conway, D. J. *Maiden, Mother, Crone: The Myth & Reality of the Triple Goddess*. Llewellyn Publications, St. Paul, Minnesota 1994.
A book that explains the many aspects of the Goddess and how the Divine is revealed through myth. This book also contains rituals and meditations designed to develop a close connection with the Goddess aspect of the Divine.

Conway, D. J. Moon *Magick: Myth & Magic, Crafts & Recipes, Rituals & Spells*. Llewellyn Publications, St. Paul, Minnesota 1995.
A book containing rituals, spells, recipes, craft instructions, and moon lore.

Cunningham, Scott. *Wicca: A Guide for the Solitary Practitioner*, Llewellyn Publications, St. Paul, Minnesota 1993.
A Wiccan primer for solitary practitioners that examines high holy days, altar set up, tool us, spell casting, and more. The book is ideal for practitioners participating in covens as well.

Currott, Phyllis, W. *Book of Shadows: A Modern Woman's Journey into the Wisdom of Witchcraft and the Magic of the Goddess*, Three Rivers Press, New York 1999.
The story of a professional woman living in New York who discovers the craft and becomes a Wiccan practitioner.

Eilers, Dana, D. *Pagans and the Law: Understand Your Rights*, ed. Lauren Manoy. Franklin Lakes, New Jersey: Career Press, 2003.
This book is a comprehensive guide to the legal rights that all Pagans have; it includes information on the American court system, child custodial issues, employment discrimination, land use, rental issues, and more.

Farrar, Stewart and Farrar, Janet. *The Witches' Bible: The Complete Witches Handbook*, Phoenix Publishing, Custer, Washington 1996.
This book is a popular guide offering information on sabbats, rituals, spell casting, and the religious significant of Magickal practices and traditions.

Galenorn, Yasmine. *Trancing the Witch's Wheel: A Guide to Magickal Meditation*. Llewellyn Publications, St. Paul, Minnesota 1997.
A book containing a series of guided meditations for developing an intensified understanding of the Divine.

Grimassi, Raven. *Wiccan Mysteries: Ancient Origins & Teachings*, Llewellyn Publications, St. Paul, Minnesota 2002.
A book that examines the historical roots of Wiccan practices, explains the meaning of various religious tenets, Magickal rites, tool and their uses, Magickal symbolism, religious ethics, and more.

Harrington, David. *The Life and Work of Scott Cunningham*, Llewellyn Publications, St. Paul, Minnesota 1973.
This book is a biography of Scott Cunningham explaining his life, his work, and his role in helping establish many of the tenets in the Wiccan religion.

Ravenwolf, Silver. *To Ride a Silver Broomstick: New Generation Witchcraft*, Llewellyn Publications, St. Paul, Minnesota 2002.
A book that explains the various traditions in The Craft, Craft practices, Magickal terms, Witch names, tool consecration and use, divinatory practices, ritual creation and performance, and more.

Ravenwolf, Silver. *To Light a Sacred Flame: Practical Witchcraft for the Millennium*, Llewellyn Publications, St. Paul, Minnesota 2002. This book contains information about candle Magick, herbs, moon Magick, runes, planetary hours, rituals, spells, and more.

Stone, Merlin. *When God Was a Woman*, Dorset Press, New York, New York 1976. A book that identifies the archaeological and historical evidence related to Goddess worship; this book examines the evolution and shift from matriarchal religions to dominant patriarchal religions around the world.

Telesco, Patricia. *A Victorian Grimoire: Romance, Enchantment, Magic.* Llewellyn Publications, St. Paul, Minnesota 1992. A book that explains Victorian symbolism in its relation to Magickal practices. This book contains a wealth of spells, rituals, and practices for seasonal celebrations, information on moon Magick, herbs, kitchen Witchery, and more.

Valiente, Doreen. *An ABC of Witchcraft Past and Present*, Phoenix Publishing, Custer, Washington 1988. A book written in an encyclopedia format explaining a variety of topics related to Witchcraft practices, beliefs, and traditions as well as historical information.

Wolfe, Amber. *In the Shadow of the Shaman: Connecting with Self, Nature & Spirit*, Llewellyn Publications, St. Paul, Minnesota 2002. This book offers information about shamanistic practices, healing, meditation, spell casting, and visualization methods.

ONLINE RESOURCES

American Civil Liberties Union
URL: http://www.aclu.org
A nonprofit organization that helps people protect their First Amendment rights, the right to due process, and other rights.

Encyclopedia Mythica™
URL: http://www.pantheon.org
A website offering encyclopedic-style entries on the Gods and Goddesses of pantheons from around the world.

Lévi, Éliphas and Waite, A. E., *Transcendental Magic, its Doctrine and Ritual*, George Redway, 1896
URL: *http://openlibrary.org/books/OL14045934M/Transcendental_magic_its_doctrine_and_ritual*.
This book is an English version of the original French work examining the theory and practice of the Magickal Arts.

Melton, J. Gordon and Lewis, James R. *Religious Requirements and Practices of Certain Selected Groups: A Handbook for Chaplains, 1993*
URL: http://onlinebooks.library.upenn.edu/webbin/book/lookupid?key=olbp23553
A book used to by the United States Army to instruct chaplains as well as the average reader about various religious beliefs and practices, including Wicca.

Occultopedia Online
URL: http://www.occultopedia.com/occult.htm.
A website with an A to Z listing of topics related to the paranormal, the supernatural, and esoteric ideas and practices.

ReligiousTolerance.org
URL: http://www.religioustolerance.org/Witchcra.htm
A site explaining the beliefs and traditions of various world religions with the intent of promoting religious tolerance.

The Malleus Maleficarum of Heinrich Kramer and James Sprenger
URL: http://www.malleusmaleficarum.org
An online text version of *The Hammer of the Witches*, a treatise published in 1947 that instructed its users on how to identify, interrogate, torture, and convict Witches.

The Witches' Voice
URL: http://www.Witchvox.com/vn/vn_index/xgroups.html
A site where visitors can find like-minded Pagans, Pagan organizations, and articles on a range of esoteric and religious topics.

ENDNOTES

CHAPTER 1

1 Charles Godfrey Leland, *Gypsy Sorcery and Fortune Telling* (London: T. Fischer Unwin, 1891), 66-67.

2 W. Chambers and R. Chambers, *Chambers's Encyclopaedia a Dictionary of Universal Knowledge for the People - Illustrated, with Maps, Steel Engravings, and Wood Cuts, revised Edition, Bel To Chi, Vol Ii* (Philadelphia: J. B. Lippincott & Co, 1883), s.v. "Witchcraft."

3-4 Charles Godfrey Leland, *Gypsy Sorcery and Fortune Telling* (London: T. Fischer Unwin, 1891), 66-67.

5 W. Chambers and R. Chambers, *Chambers's Encyclopaedia a Dictionary of Universal Knowledge for the People - Illustrated, with Maps, Steel Engravings, and Wood Cuts, revised Edition, Bel To Chi, Vol Ii* (Philadelphia: J. B. Lippincott & Co, 1883), s.v. "Witchcraft."

6 F. Kluge and F. Lutz, *English Etymology: A Select Glossary Serving as an Introduction to the History of the English Language* (Boston: D.C. Health & Co., Publishers, 1898), s.v. "Witch."

7-8 William W Smith, *A Complete Etymology of the English Language: Containing the Anglo-Saxon, French, Dutch, German, Welsh, Danish, Gothic, Swedish, Gaelic, Italian, Latin ... Accurately Spelled, Accented, and Defined* (Chicago: A. S. Barnes and Company, 1872), s.v. "Wician."

9 Charles Godfrey Leland, *Gypsy Sorcery and Fortune Telling* (London: T. Fischer Unwin, 1891), 66-67.

10 Plato, *Talks with Socrates about Life: Translations from the Gorgias and The Republic* (New York: Charles Scribner's Sons, 1887), 120-136.

[11] Robert Sullivan LL.D, T.C.D., *A Dictionary of Derivations or An Introduction to Etymology: On a New Plan*, 12th ed. (London: Dublin: Sullivan, Brothers, 1870), s.v. "Pagan."

[12-13] Noah Webster, *A Dictionary of the English Language, Explanatory, Pronouncing, Etymological, and Synonymous* (Philadelphia: J. B. Lippincott & Company, 1875), s.v. "Pagan."

[14] Hensleigh Wedgwood, *A Dictionary of English Etymology*, 3rd ed. (New York: Macmillan, 1878), s.v. "Pagan."

[15-16] *Oxford English Dictionary Online*, 2004 ed. (Oxford University Press, May 2004), s.v. "Cult," http://dictionary.oed.com/cgi/entry/50055591 (accessed August 24, 2010).

[17] *Oxford English Dictionary Online*, 1989 ed. (Oxford University Press, May 2004), s.v. "Magic," http://dictionary.oed.com/cgi/entry/00299414 (accessed August 24, 2010).

[18] Geoffrey Chaucer, *The Prologue to the Canterbury Tales*, ed. E. F. Willoughby M.D. (New York: Maynard, Merrill, & Co., 1881), 73.

[19-20] *Oxford English Dictionary Online*, 1989 ed. (Oxford University Press, May 2004), s.v. "Magic," http://dictionary.oed.com/cgi/entry/00299414 (accessed August 24, 2010).

[21] *Oxford English Dictionary Online*, 1989 ed. (Oxford University Press, May 2004), s.v. "New Age," http://dictionary.oed.com/cgi/entry/00310680 (accessed August 24, 2010).

[22] William Dwight Whitney Ph.D., LL.D, The *Century Dictionary and Cyclopedia: A Work of Universal Reference in All Departments of Knowledge with a New Atlas of the World Volume II* (New York: The Century Company, 1906), s.v. "Convent."

[23] Friedrich Kluge and Frederick Lutz, *English Etymology: A Select Glossary Serving as an Introduction to the History of the English Language* (Boston: D. C. Heath & Co., Publishers, 1898), s.v. "War."

[24] Friedrich Kluge and Frederick Lutz, *English Etymology: A Select Glossary Serving as an Introduction to the History of the English Language* (Boston: D. C. Heath & Co., Publishers, 1898), s.v. "Warlock."

[25-26] Charles G Herbermann Ph.D., LL.D, et al., eds., *The Catholic Encyclopedia: An International Work of Reference on the Constitution, Doctrine, Discipline, and History of the Catholic Church Volume 11* (New York: The Encyclopedia Press Inc., 1911), s.v. "None."

[27] Exod. 20:3 (RSV).

[28] Deut. 18:9-11 (RSV).

[29] William E Addis and Thomas Arnold M.A., *A Catholic Dictionary: Containing Some Account of the Doctrine, Discipline, Rites, Ceremonies, Councils, and Religious Orders of the Catholic Church,*

rev. ed., ed. Rev. T.B. Scannell B.D. (London: Kegan Paul, Tkench, Trubner & Co. Ltd, 1893), s.v. "Witchcraft."
[30] Lev. Leviticus:19:28 (RSV).

CHAPTER 2

[1] W. Chambers and R. Chambers, *Chambers's Encyclopaedia a Dictionary of Universal Knowledge Vol Viii* (Philadelphia: J. B. Lippincott & Co, 1882), s.v. "Pentacle."
[2] William Jones F.S.A., *Credulities Past and Present: Including the Sea and Seamen, Miners, Amulets and Talismans, Rings, Word and Letter Divination, Numbers, Trials, Exorcising and Blessing of Animals, Birds, Eggs, and Luck* (London: Chatto & Windus, 1898), 8-10.
[3] Heinrich Cornelius Agrippa, *Three Books of Occult Philosophy*, trans. J. F. London (1555; repr., R.W. for Gregory Moule, 1651), 188-190.
[4] Eliphas Levi, *Dogme et Rituel de la Haute Magie: Part II: The Ritual of Transcendental Magic*, trans. A. E. Waite (England: Rider & Company, 1896), 35-37, http://www.holybooks.com/wp-content/uploads/2010/05/Transcendental-Magic-Its-Doctrine-and-Ritual1-1.8-MB.pdf (accessed August 11, 2010).
[5] Stephen W Massil and Anne J. Kershen, *The Jewish Yearbook: An Annual Record of Matters Jewish*, 2nd ed., ed. Joseph Jacobs (London: Greenberg & Co., 1896), 167.
[6] William Wiberforce Rand, *Dictionary of the Holy Bible*, rev. ed. (New York: American Tract Society, 1886), s.v. "Devil."
[7] John Gregorson Campbell, *Witchcraft and Second Sight in the Highlands and Islands of Scotland: Tales and Traditions Collected Entirely from Oral Sources* (Glasgow: James MacLehose and Sons, 1902), 34-41.
[8] Edwin Greenlaw, William M Dey, and George Howe, *"Witches as Cats," Studies in Philology: A Quarterly Journal Published by the University of North Carolina* 16 (1919): 233-235.
[9-10] Georgia Allen Peck, *"The Survival of Celestial Superstitions," The Chautauquan: A Monthly Magazine*, April 1894, 751-753.
[11] Israel Smith Clare, *The Unrivaled History of the World: Containing a Full and Complete Record of the Human Race, vol. 3 of Midiæval History* (Chicago: Unrivaled Publishing Co., 1889), 50-62.
[12] Henry Charles Lea LL.D, *A History of The Inquisition of the Middle Ages* (New York: The MacMillan Company, 1922), 3:501-502.
[13] *Oxford English Dictionary Online*, 2010 ed. (Oxford University Press, 2004), s.v. "Necromancy," http://dictionary.oed.com/cgi/entry/00322322 (accessed August 24, 2010).

[14] George Ripley and Charles A. Dana, eds., *The American Cyclopædia: A Popular Dictionary of General Knowledge Volume X* (New York: D. Appleton and Company, 1875), s.v. "Necromancy."

[15] U.S. Constitution, amend. 1.

[16] Dana D Eilers, *Pagans and the Law: Understand Your Rights*, ed. Lauren Manoy (Franklin Lakes, New Jersey: Career Press, 2003), 55-80.

[17] Dana D Eilers, *"Paganism and the Law: Some Brief Points for Modern Pagans,"* The Witches'Voice Inc., http://www.Witchvox.com/white/paganismandlaw.html (accessed August 11, 2010).

[18] Dana D Eilers, *Pagans and the Law: Understand Your Rights*, ed. Lauren Manoy (Franklin Lakes, New Jersey: Career Press, 2003), 70-75.

[19] Don Branum Sgt, "Academy Chapel to Add Outdoor Circle to Worship Areas," *The Official Site of the U.S. Air Force*, http://www.af.mil/news/story.asp?id=123188608 (accessed August 11, 2010).

[20] African Eye, "Principal accused of Witchcraft," *News24.com* (Cape Town), April 8, 2010, http://www.news24.com/SouthAfrica/News/Principal-accused-of-Witchcraft-20100804 (accessed August 25, 2010).

[21] Amira Agarib, "'Witchcraft'psychiatrist nabbed by Dubai police," *Khaleej Times Online* (Dubai), August 5, 2010, http://www.khaleejtimes.com/DisplayArticle.asp?xfile=data/theuae/2010/August/theuae_August155.xml&section=theuae&col= (accessed August 25, 2010).

CHAPTER 3

[1] William L Davidson M.A. LL.D., *Theism as Grounded in Human Nature, Historically and Critically Handled: Being the Burnett Lectures for 1892 and 1893* (London: Longmans, Green, and Co., 1893), 135-140.

[2] Scott Cunningham, Wicca: *A Guide for the Solitary Practitioner* (St. Paul, Minnesota: Llewellyn Publications, 1993), 159.

[3-4] Silver Ravenwolf, *To Ride a Silver Broomstick: New Generation Witchcraft* (St. Paul, Minnesota: Llewellyn Publications, 2004), 6-8.

[5] Scott Cunningham, *Wicca: A Guide for the Solitary Practitioner* (St. Paul, Minnesota: Llewellyn Publications, 1993), 152-153.

[6] Scott Cunningham, *Cunningham's Encyclopedia of Magical Herbs* (St. Paul, Minnesota: Llewellyn, 2005), 10.

[7-8] Silver Ravenwolf, *To Ride a Silver Broomstick: New Generation*

*Witch*craft (St. Paul, Minnesota: Llewellyn Publications, 2004), 284.

[9-10] Ed Fitch, *Magical Rites from the Crystal Well* (St. Paul, Minnesota: Llewellyn Publications, 2000), 2.

[11-12] Raven Grimassi, *Encyclopedia of Wicca & Witchcraft* (St. Paul, Minnesota: Llewellyn Publications, 2000), 435-437.

[13-14] Amber K, *Covencraft: Witchcraft for Three or More* (St. Paul, Minnesota: Llewellyn Publications, 2003), 4-5.

[15] *Oxford English Dictionary Online*, 1989 ed. (Oxford University Press, June 2010), s.v. "Rede," http://dictionary.oed.com/cgi/entry/50199971 (accessed August 24, 2010).

[15] Hate Crime Graffiti, personal photograph by Philip Gadreau, May-June 2008.

CHAPTER 4

[1] Kaitlin McCarthy, David Romero, and Bill Diven, "APD Arrests Wiccan Follower for Murder," *KRQE News 13*, March 23, 2010, http://www.krqe.com/dpp/news/crime/apd-arrests-wiccan-follower-for-murder (accessed July 24, 2010).

[2] Pete Williams, "Feds: Militia Members Sought to Spark Uprising," *Msnbc.com*, March 30, 2010, http://www.msnbc.msn.com/id/36075836/ns/us_news-security (accessed July 24, 2010).

[3] Linda StCyr, "Wiccan Blood Oath Blamed for Murder of Everett, Wash. Woman," *Associated Content*, February 9, 2010, http://www.associatedcontent.com/article/2683845/Wiccan_blood_oath_blamed_for_murder.html (accessed July 24, 2010).

[4] *WMUR New Hampshire*, "Grave-Robbing Could Be Linked to Ritual Beliefs," November 6, 2007, http://www.wmur.com/news/14526508/detail.html (accessed July 24, 2010).

BIBLIOGRAPHY

Addis, William E, and Thomas Arnold, M.A. *A Catholic Dictionary: Containing Some Account of the Doctrine, Discipline, Rites, Ceremonies, Councils, and Religious Orders of the Catholic Church.* rev. ed. Edited by Rev. T.B. Scannell B.D. London: Kegan Paul, Tkench, Trubner & Co. Ltd, 1893. S.v. "Witchcraft."

African Eye. "Principal accused of witchcraft." *News24. com* (Cape Town), April 8, 2010. http://www.news24.com/SouthAfrica/News/Principal-accused-of-witchcraft-20100804 (accessed August 25, 2010).

Agarib, Amira. "'Witchcraft'psychiatrist nabbed by Dubai police." *Khaleej Times Online* (Dubai), August 5, 2010. http://www.khaleejtimes.com/DisplayArticle.asp?xfile=data/theuae/2010/August/theuae_August155.xml&section=theuae&col= (accessed August 25, 2010).

Agrippa, Heinrich Cornelius. *Three Books of Occult Philosophy.* Translated by J. F. London. 1555. Reprint, R.W. for Gregory Moule, 1651.

Branum, Don, Sgt. "Academy Chapel to Add Outdoor Circle to Worship Areas." The Official Site of the U.S. Air Force. http://www.af.mil/news/story.asp?id=123188608 (accessed August 11, 2010).

Campbell, John Gregorson. *Witchcraft and Second Sight in the Highlands and Islands of Scotland: Tales and Traditions Collected Entirely from Oral Sources.* Glasgow: James MacLehose and Sons, 1902.

Chambers, W, and R Chambers. *Chambers's Encyclopaedia a Dictionary of Universal Knowledge for the People - Illustrated, with Maps, Steel Engravings, and Wood Cuts, Revised Edition, Bel To Chi, Vol Ii*. Philadelphia: J. B. Lippincott & Co, 1883. S.v. "Witchcraft."

— — —. *Chambers's Encyclopaedia a Dictionary of Universal Knowledge Vol Viii*. Philadelphia: J. B. Lippincott & Co, 1882. S.v. "Pentacle."

Chaucer, Geoffrey. *The Prologue to the Canterbury Tales*. Edited by E. F. Willoughby M.D. New York: Maynard, Merrill, & Co., 1881.

Clare, Israel Smith. *The Unrivaled History of the World: Containing a Full and Complete Record of the Human Race*. Vol. 3 of *Midiæval History*. Chicago: Unrivaled Publishing Co., 1889.

Cunningham, Scott. *Cunningham's Encyclopedia of Magical Herbs*. St. Paul, Minnesota: Llewellyn, 2005.

— — —. *Wicca: A Guide for the Solitary Practitioner*. St. Paul, Minnesota: Llewellyn Publications, 1993.

Davidson, William L, M.A. LL.D. *Theism as Grounded in Human Nature, Historically and Critically Handled : Being the Burnett Lectures for 1892 and 1893*. London: Longmans, Green, and Co., 1893.

Eilers, Dana D. "Paganism and the Law: Some Brief Points for Modern Pagans." The Witches' Voice Inc. http://www.witchvox.com/white/paganismandlaw.html (accessed August 11, 2010).

— — —. *Pagans and the Law: Understand Your Rights*. Edited by Lauren Manoy. Franklin Lakes, New Jersey: Career Press, 2003.

Fitch, Ed. *Magical Rites from the Crystal Well*. St. Paul, Minnesota: Llewellyn Publications, 2000.

Greenlaw, Edwin, William M Dey, and George Howe. "Witches as Cats." *Studies in Philology: A Quarterly Journal Published by the University of North Carolina* 16 (1919): 233-235.

Grimassi, Raven. *Encyclopedia of Wicca & Witchcraft*. St. Paul, Minnesota: Llewellyn Publications, 2000.

Hate Crime Graffitti, personal photograph by Phillip Gaudreau, May-June 2008.

Herbermann, Charles G Ph.D., LL.D, Edward A Pace Ph.D. D.D, Condé B. Pallen Ph.D LL.D, Thomas J Shahan D.D., and John J Wynne S.J., eds. *The Catholic Encyclopedia: An International Work of Reference on the Constitution, Doctrine, Discipline, and History of the Catholic Church Volume 11*. New York: The Encyclopedia Press Inc., 1911. S.v. "None."

Jones, William, F.S.A. *Credulities Past and Present: Including the Sea and Seamen, Miners, Amulets and Talismans, Rings, Word and Letter Divination, Numbers, Trials, Exorcising and Blessing of Animals, Birds, Eggs, and Luck.* London: Chatto & Windus, 1898.

K, Amber. *Covencraft: Witchcraft for Three or More.* St. Paul, Minnesota: Llewellyn Publications, 2003.

Kluge, F, and F Lutz. *English Etymology: A Select Glossary Serving as an Introduction to the History of the English Language.* Boston: D. C. Heath & Co., Publishers, 1898. S.v. "Witch."

Kluge, Friedrich, and Frederick Lutz. *English Etymology: A Select Glossary Serving as an Introduction to the History of the English Language.* Boston: D. C. Heath & Co., Publishers, 1898. S.v. "War."

— — —. *English Etymology: A Select Glossary Serving as an Introduction to the History of the English Language.* Boston: D. C. Heath & Co., Publishers, 1898. S.v. "Warlock."

Lea, Henry Charles, LL.D. *A History of The Inquisition of the Middle Ages.* Vol. 3. New York: The MacMillan Company, 1922.

Leland, Charles Godfrey. *Gypsy Sorcery and Fortune Telling.* London: T. Fischer Unwin, 1891.

Lévi, Éliphas. *Dogme et Rituel de la Haute Magie: Part II: The Ritual of Transcendental Magic.* Translated by A. E. Waite. England: Rider & Company, 1896. http://www.holybooks.com/wp-content/up loads/2010/05/Transcendental-Magic-Its-Doctrine-and-Ritual1-1.8-MB.pdf (accessed August 11, 2010).

Massil, Stephen W, and Anne J. Kershen. *The Jewish Yearbook: An Annual Record of Matters Jewish.* 2nd ed. Edited by Joseph Jacobs. London: Greenberg & Co., 1896.

McCarthy, Kaitlin, David Romero, and Bill Diven. "APD Arrests Wiccan Follower for Murder." *KRQE News 13*, March 23, 2010. http://www.krqe.com/dpp/news/crime/apd-arrests-wiccan-follower-for-murder (accessed July 24, 2010).

Miller, Carlin DeGuerin. "http://www.cbsnews.com/8301-504083_162-20001162-504083.html." *CBS News: Crimesider*, March 25, 2010. http://www.cbsnews.com/8301-504083_162-20001162-504083.html (accessed July 24, 2010).

Oxford English Dictionary Online. 2004 ed. Oxford University Press, May 2004. S.v. "Cult." http://dictionary.oed.com/cgi/entry/50055591 (accessed August 24, 2010).

Oxford English Dictionary Online. 1989 ed. Oxford University Press, June 2010. S.v. "Rede." http://dictionary.oed.com/cgi/entry/50199971 (accessed August 24, 2010).

Oxford English Dictionary Online. 1989 ed. Oxford University Press, May 2004. S.v. "New Age." http://dictionary.oed.com/cgi/entry/00310680 (accessed August 24, 2010).

Oxford English Dictionary Online. 2010 ed. Oxford University Press, 2004. S.v. "Necromancy." http://dictionary.oed.com/cgi/entry/00322322 (accessed August 24, 2010).

Peck, Georgia Allen. "The Survival of Celestial Superstitions." *The Chautauquan: A Monthly Magazine*, April 1894, 751-753.

Plato. *Talks with Socrates about Life: Translations from The Gorgias and The Republic.* New York: Charles Scribner's Sons, 1887.

Rand, William Wiberforce. *Dictionary of the Holy Bible.* rev. ed. New York: American Tract Society, 1886. S.v. "Devil."

Ravenwolf, Silver. *To Ride a Silver Broomstick: New Generation Witchcraft.* St. Paul, Minnesota: Llewellyn Publications, 2004.

— — —. *To Ride a Silver Broomstick: New Generation Witchcraft.* St. Paul, Minnesota: Llewellyn Publications, 2004.

Ripley, George, and Charles A. Dana, eds. *The American Cyclopædia: A Popular Dictionary of General Knowledge Volume X.* New York: D. Appleton and Company, 1875. S.v. "Necromancy."

Skeat, Walter William. *An Etymological Dictionary of the English Language.* 3rd ed. London: Henry Frowde, M.A., 1898. S.v. "Magic."

Smith, William W. *A Complete Etymology of the English Language: Containing the Anglo-Saxon, French, Dutch, German, Welsh, Danish, Gothic, Swedish, Gaelic, Italian, Latin ... Accurately Spelled, Accented, and Defined.* Chicago: A. S. Barnes and Company, 1872. S.v. "Witch."

— — —. *A Complete Etymology of the English Language: Containing the Anglo-Saxon, French, Dutch, German, Welsh, Danish, Gothic, Swedish, Gaelic, Italian, Latin ... Accurately Spelled, Accented, and Defined.* Chicago: A. S. Barnes and Company, 1872. S.v. "Wician."

StCyr, Linda. "Wiccan Blood Oath Blamed for Murder of Everett, Wash. Woman." *Associated Content*, February 9, 2010. http://www.associatedcontent.com/article/2683845/Wiccan_blood_oath_blamed_for_murder.html (accessed July 24, 2010).

Sullivan, Robert, LL.D, T.C.D. *A Dictionary of Derivations or An Introduction to Etymology: On a New Plan.* 12th ed. London: Dublin: Sullivan, Brothers, 1870. S.v. "Pagan."

Valiente, Doreen. *Witchcraft For Tomorrow*. Blaine, Washington: Phoenix Publishing, 1978.

Webster, Noah. *A Dictionary of the English Language, Explanatory, Pronouncing, Etymological, and Synonymous*. Philadelphia: J. B. Lippincott & Company, 1875. S.v. "Pagan."

Wedgwood, Hensleigh. *A Dictionary of English Etymology*. 3rd ed. New York: Macmillan, 1878. S.v. "Pagan."

Whitney, William Dwight, Ph.D., LL.D. *The Century Dictionary and Cyclopedia: A Work of Universal Reference in All Departments of Knowledge with a New Atlas of the World Volume II*. New York: The Century Company, 1906. S.v. "Convent."

Williams, Pete. "Feds: Militia Members Sought to Spark Uprising." *Msnbc.com*, March 30, 2010. http://www.msnbc.msn.com/id/36075836/ns/us_news-security (accessed July 24, 2010).

WMUR New Hampshire. "Grave-Robbing Could Be Linked To Ritual Beliefs." November 6, 2007. http://www.wmur.com/news/14526508/detail.html (accessed July 24, 2010).

INDEX

Necromancy, 71, 152
New Age, 16-17, 152
Nudity, *see Skyclad.*

Occult, 13-14, 16, 20, 29, 31, 55, 81,
    133-135, 137-138, 143, 151-152,
    156
Oimelc, *see Candlemas.*
Ostara, *see Spring Equinox.*
Ouija Boards, 76-77, 108, 152
Out of Body Experience, *see Astral
    Projection.*

Palmistry, 108, 153
Pan, 58, 61
Pentacle, 82, 153
Pentagram, 54-57, 82, 153
Principles of Belief, 45, 72, 111
Psychic, 19, 66, 72, 76, 108, 110-111,
    119, 127, 149, 153, 155
Psychometry, 108, 110, 153

Reflexology, 108, 153
Reiki, 108, 153
Reincarnation, 37, 55, 116, 134, 153
Ritual, 17, 23, 31-32, 45, 51-54, 56-57,
    60, 66-67, 69, 70, 71-72, 75, 76,
    86-90, 92, 95, 97, 99-101, 104, 108,
    118, 130, 135-136, 139, 142, 148,
    149, 150-155
Rule of Three, *see Three-Fold Law.*

Sabbat, 17, 27, 56, 86, 91-96, 98-100,
    102, 104, 114, 149, 154, 115
Sacrifice, 15, 53, 65, 70, 79, 86, 141
Salem, Massachusetts, 82-83, 154
Samhain, 23, 36-37, 71, 91, 92, 97,
    101, 143
Satan, 18, 32, 33, 36, 56-67, 59, 60-62,
    66, 71, 112, 123-124, 154
Satanist, 18, 20, 51, 60, 66, 154
Scrying, 107-108, 154
Seal of Solomon, 57
Séance, 76-77, 108-109, 154
Self-Delusion, 134-136
Sex Magick, 66, 67, 68, 154
Sin, 10, 32, 36-38, 66, 68, 129, 154

Skyclad, 66-67, 154, 155
Solitary witch, 88, 121, 155
Spells, 20-23, 45, 70, 74-75, 77-78, 90,
    94-96, 106-107, 110, 115, 121, 139-
    140, 145, 151, 155
Spirit Communication, 76, 105, 108,
    109, 121, 155
Spring Equinox, 94-97, 141
Stag King, 48, 58
Star of David, 57
Statues, 46, 89, 106, 148
Stone, Merlin, 159
Summer Solstice, 93-94, 97-101
Summer's End, *see Samhain.*
Sword, 52, 53, 89, 139, 155

Tarot, 50, 108, 132, 150, 155
Tattoos, 33, 36
Teenagers, 28-29, 72
Television, 6, 23-24, 122
Tenets, 21, 25, 28-29, 39, 42, 47, 70,
    77, 110-112, 130, 137, 141-142
Thirteen Goals of a Witch, 45, 110
Three-fold Law of Return, *see Three-
    Fold Law.*
Three-Fold Law, 112, 115-116, 153, 155
Trees, 49

Valiente, Doreen, 107, 114
Vegans, 78
Vegetarians, 78
Visualization, 52-53, 88, 104, 110,
    118, 136, 142, 155

Warlock, 18, 155
Wheel of the Year, 91, 97, 10, 155
Wiccan Rede, 22, 78, 106, 114, 141,
    156
Wiccaning, 104, 156
Witch hunts, 42, 83, 94, 156
Witch Trials, 82-83, 154
Witches' Creed, The, 114
Witches' Rede of Chivalry, 112
Witches' Rede, The 112, 114
Witching Hour, The, 19

Yule, 93-94, 95, 99, 101

PATRICIA GARDNER

Patricia Gardner is a Witch and the High Priestess of the Dragon Warrior's of ISIS Coven in Upstate, New York. She is the co-founder and co-director of ISIS Paranormal Investigations, and she co-hosts the *ISIS Paranormal Radio* Show. She has had publications appear on Isisinvestigations.com, Unexplained-Mysteries.com, Ghost-mysteries.com, and Haunted-Voices.com. Her radio, television, and film appearances include *Alabama ParaSpiritual Talk Radio Show, the X-Zone Radio Show with Rob McConnell, Haunted Voices Radio, The Morning Rush Show on Fly 92.3 FM, The Soul Salon, Paranormal Radio with Captain Jack, Psychic Wisdom with David James, Encounters with the Paranormal,* and *The Gut & Bone Show.* Patricia has also been featured in *Chat: It's Fate, 14 Degrees: A Paranormal Documentary,* and Discovery Channel's *A Haunting.*

ANGELA KAUFMAN

Angela Kaufman is a Witch, Priestess in the Dragon Warriors of Isis Coven, and a Licensed Clinical Social Worker with over five years of experience working with individuals with mental health and substance abuse issues. She is also a professional Tarot card reader and owner of Moonlight Tarot. She has had several articles published on ISIS Paranormal Investigations. She is a psychic artist for the latter ghost investigation group, and she has had publications appear in *Wisdom Magazine*. Her radio, television, and film appearances include *The Morning Rush Show* on *Fly 92.3 FM, 14 Degrees: A Paranormal Documentary,* Discovery Channel's *A Haunting,* and *The ISIS Paranormal Radio Show.*

DAYNA WINTERS

Dayna Winters is a Witch, Priestess in the Dragon Warriors of Isis Coven, and a freelance writer. She earned an Associate in Arts from Hudson Valley Community College, and later graduated *magna cum laude* from Sage College with a Bachelor of Arts in English. Dayna is one of the co-founders and co-directors of ISIS Paranormal Investigations in Upstate New York, and the co-host of *ISIS Paranormal Radio*. Her publications have appeared in *Threads Magazine, Crescent Magazine, Blood Moon Rising Magazine*, and *The Journal for the Academic Study of Magic*. Her radio interviews include *Alabama ParaSpiritual Talk Radio Show*, the X-Zone Radio Show with Rob McConnell, *Haunted Voices Radio, The Morning Rush Show on Fly 92.3 FM, Paranormal Radio with Captain Jack*, among others. Dayna was also featured in *Chat: It's Fate, 14 Degrees: A Paranormal Documentary*, and Discovery Channel's *A Haunting*.